Out of print
First Am. Edition
Review copy

#170-1728

W9-CNV-436

The Amazing Mississippi

BOOKS BY

WILLARD PRICE

The Amazing Mississippi
Incredible Africa
Roaming Britain
Adventures in Paradise
Journey by Junk
The Amazing Amazon
I Cannot Rest from Travel
Roving South
Key to Japan
Japan and the Son of Heaven
Japan's Islands of Mystery
Japan Rides the Tiger
Barbarian (a novel)
Children of the Rising Sun
Pacific Adventure
Ancient Peoples at New Tasks
The Negro Around the World
America's Influence in the Orient

FOR BOYS:

Whale Adventure
Volcano Adventure
Underwater Adventure
South Sea Adventure
Amazon Adventure

WILLARD PRICE

The Amazing Mississippi

WITH 48 PAGES OF PHOTOGRAPHS

The John Day Company
New York

FIRST AMERICAN EDITION, 1963

©1962 by Willard Price. All rights reserved. This book, or parts thereof, must not be reproduced in any form without permission. Published by The John Day Company, 62 West 45th Street, New York 36, New York, and simultaneously in Canada by Longmans Canada Limited, Toronto.

Library of Congress Catalogue
Card Number: 62-15134

MANUFACTURED IN THE UNITED STATES OF AMERICA

TO
GERRY HAWKINS

Contents

Illustrations (photographs by the author and Mary Virginia Price) are to be found following pages 54, 86 and 158.

Acknowledgment

Acknowledgment is due to the National Geographic Society for substantial co-operation in this project.

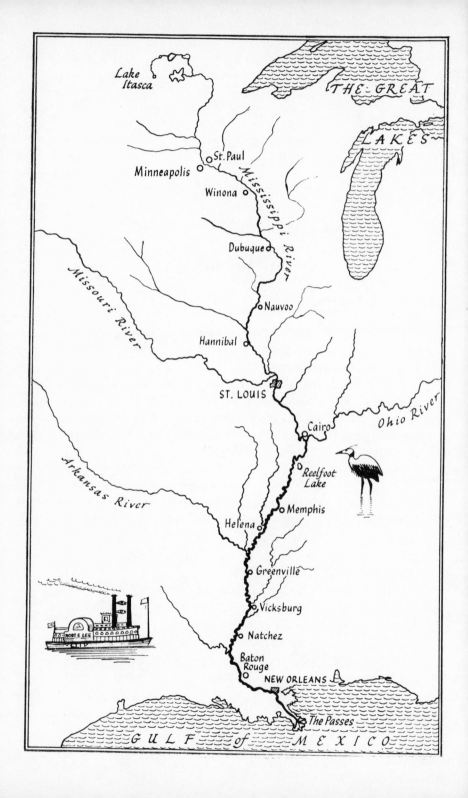

I

Backbone of America

HE STOOD HIS GROUND, snarling, trying to make up his mind what to do. I blocked his path. The river behind him cut off his retreat.

I took another step forward. Like a flash, the bobcat wheeled, fled to the river's edge, spanned the river in one great leap and disappeared in the forest.

The river was the Mississippi. Since we all know that the Mississippi thinks nothing of being a mile wide and in flood may reach a width of eighty miles, to leap across it would seem to be a feat possible only to Paul Bunyan's mythical Blue Ox.

But at the point where we stood gazing across the stream after the vanished bobcat, the Mississippi was only ten feet wide. It was just a babbling brook – with very little to babble about, for it was not old enough to know much. Two minutes ago it was born. A hundred yards back it had issued from Lake Itasca past a wooden marker designating this spot as the source of the Mississippi.

Forest-girdled Lake Itasca lies in northern Minnesota not very far from the Canadian border. Its discoverer, Henry Schoolcraft, fixed upon it as the true source of the Mississippi. Searching for some name that would suggest True Head, he came upon the Latin words *veritas caput*. That would be too long a name – so, with skilful surgery, he chopped off the first and last syllables and came out with Itasca.

It had a pleasantly Indian sound. In fact, ethnologists have ever since been trying to trace it back to the Chippewa language. One went so far as to imagine it the name of the tribal god's unhappy daughter whose falling tears formed the lake.

But the question was settled once and for all when a scholar happened upon a letter written by Schoolcraft to a Galena newspaper on 25 July 1832, twelve days after the discovery, stating plainly that the name Itasca was devised from *veritas caput*. This habit, by the way, of shaping names from Latin origins was quite the fashion in those days.

But is Itasca the true head of the Mississippi? Sceptically, we explored the lake shore in our canoe. At the far end we found the source of the source of the Mississippi – a small stream flowing into Lake Itasca.

The stream was too shallow for the canoe, so we picked up the craft and portaged a few hundred yards to find that the creek flowed out of a smaller lake which appeared on the map as Elk Lake. Again we explored the shoreline and found an incoming stream from Little Elk Lake.

It illustrates the futility of naming any one patch of moisture the true source of a river. Where should one stop? The stream entering Little Elk comes from a pond higher up, and the pond from a spring still higher. According to the humorous speculations of author Holling C. Holling, above this spring is a tree, and on top of the tree sits a crow with the rain pouring upon its back and running off both ends; one has only to learn which end of the crow is higher and that is the true source of the Mississippi.

The way out of this absurdity was offered by a ranger we met in Itasca State Park bordering the lake.

'The truth is,' he said, 'that all the lakes in the Itasca region are interrelated by underground seepages and springs so that it is impossible to specify any one as *the* source of the

Mississippi. The whole system is one big sponge. You can only say that the source is the Itasca basin.'

The signpost which pinpoints one spot as the source of the Mississippi makes another doubtful assumption. It announces the length of the Mississippi from this point to the mouth as 2,552 miles.

The fact is no one knows the length of the Mississippi – and if he knew today he would have to revise his figure tomorrow. The river channel is constantly changing. Blocked by a sandbar, it may go several miles out of its way around islands. Where it makes a thirty-mile loop it may suddenly gather its strength and cut through the neck of the loop, reducing the river's length by thirty miles. It is the crookedest great waterway in the world and the most fickle. Even the Army Engineers whose business it is to control the river cautiously use the word 'approximately' when they estimate its present length at 2,434 miles.

The fame of the Mississippi draws many visitors to the spot where the infant river creeps over the lip of Lake Itasca and starts on its long journey to the sea. Boulders serve as stepping-stones across the stream, and if you slip from one of them the result is not too serious, for the rivulet is ordinarily only ankle deep. It is hard to imagine that this puling infant is to become the Father of Waters.

This timid little creek will grow to be the greatest river in North America; the greatest in the world with the possible exception of the Amazon. It will gather to itself more than 100,000 tributaries, large and small. It and its affluents will provide 15,700 miles of inland navigation.

The vast Mississippi water-web will drain forty per cent of the United States, not to mention 13,000 square miles of Canada. It will draw water from thirty-one states, and some of the fingers of its longest arm, the Missouri, will reach seventy miles into a Canadian province.

Its drainage area will stretch to a maximum of 1,900 miles

in longitude and 1,400 miles in latitude and will cover 1,243,700 square miles.

That, as Mark Twain chose to interpret it, 'is as great as the combined areas of England, Wales, Scotland, Ireland, France, Spain, Portugal, Germany, Austria, Italy and Turkey'.

The river exacts tribute from states as far east as New York and as far west as Montana. No wonder that the explorers, hearing Indian stories of the great river, dreamed that it would carry them to China.

Some authorities consider it the longest river on the globe, measuring from the source of the Missouri to the Gulf, about 4,200 miles – but, again, this is a variable figure due to the river's habit of stretching and contracting like a temperamental caterpillar.

'When God made the world,' said the Mississippi orator, S. S. Prentiss, 'he had a large amount of surplus water which he turned loose and told to go where it pleased; it has been going where it pleased ever since and that is the Mississippi River.'

God's surplus pours into the Gulf of Mexico at the rate of 785,000 million cubic yards a year. It delivers three times as much water as the mighty St Lawrence, twenty-five times as much as the majestic Rhine, 338 times as much as the Thames.

The Creator seems also to have had more mud than he could use. The Mississippi has been industriously carrying it off at the rate of five hundred million tons a year.

Long ages of such mud-slinging have had an astounding result. Enough mud has been thrown out to make a country the size of Portugal. Generous portions of Missouri, Tennessee, Arkansas, Mississippi and Louisiana came from Minnesota, Iowa, the Dakotas, Montana and Canada. That is a debt the South owes to the North!

The Mississippi once poured into the sea at Cairo, Illinois.

The Gulf of Mexico extended up to this point. Deposits of sediment pushed the Gulf farther and farther south, laid down a mud plain twenty to eighty miles wide and lengthened the river by some thousand miles.

Other great American rivers such as the Columbia, the Colorado and the Rio Grande are so hampered in their flow by man's devices that their delivery of sediment is negligible. The Colorado, for example, lays down most of its burden in Lake Mead, blocked by Hoover Dam. The Rio Grande carries silt but lazily drops most of it before reaching salt water. Huge dams discourage the Columbia.

While there are many dams on the Upper Mississippi, there is not one such obstruction between Illinois and the Gulf. The turbid Missouri, the bulky Ohio, the red-earth Arkansas and a dozen other great silt carriers pour their sediment into the Mississippi, which carries it at a fairly steady pace of about six knots to the sea.

Captain Marryat called the Mississippi 'the Great Sewer'. There is truth in it, yet it is not a good name. Any riverman would resent it, for it does not suggest the grandeur, the glory, the thrill of the magnificent river. The Indians honoured the stream by describing it as half god, half devil. The Ojibways called it Misisipi, from *misi*, big, and *sipi*, river.

Imaginative French explorers translated the name as Father of Waters. This error, writes historian George R. Stewart, 'led to millions of American schoolchildren being taught the falsehood that Mississippi meant Father of Waters. It was a falsehood not only about a single name, but about Indians in general – for such a figure of speech would hardly have been used for a river'.

Whatever its origin, 'Father of Waters' does suggest the supremacy of the Mississippi among rivers. So does the Indians' nickname, 'Old Big Strong', and the negroes' 'Old Man River', and 'Ole Miss'. The Indians and negroes did better than the early explorers who dubbed it variously

'Conception River', 'Baude River', 'Colbert River' and 'Río del Espíritu Santo'. Fortunately and appropriately time has obliterated all but the Indian 'Mississippi' – a noble name though, as we are forced to spell it, unnecessarily sandbarred with s's and p's.

The Mississippi is America's backbone from which proliferating spinal nerves pass to the sense organs, muscles and glands of the body politic from the Rockies to the Atlantic. The agricultural mid-West and the industrial East are linked with New Orleans and, through that second greatest of all America's export outlets, with all the world.

The greatest such port, New York, is also a part of the system. From the Mississippi by way of the Great Lakes and canals, cargo may be waterborne all the way to New York or Montreal, there to be trans-shipped across the Atlantic or around the globe.

During the steamboat era Mississippi tonnage was greater than the entire tonnage transported by all the ships of the British Empire. In 1849 there were a thousand big packets plying the river. The end came rather suddenly. After the Civil War the steamboats were eclipsed by the railroads.

The Mississippi was dead. Progress had passed it by. No one dreamed it would ever come to life again. It was only natural to suppose that slow transport must always give way to rapid transport. Improved roads allowed trucks to compete with the railroads. Both began to yield to the aeroplane. There could surely be no return to the plodding riverboat.

But during the two world wars the government, as an emergency measure to relieve transportation congestion, revived river traffic. From December 1941 until 15 August 1945, the amount of petroleum alone transported on American inland waterways (mostly on the Mississippi network) was the equivalent of seven million carloads or 72,732 freight trains of one hundred cars each.

'If our waterways rendered no services beyond that of

transporting petroleum and its products during the war,'
stated the Office of Defence Transportation, 'they would
have amply justified their improved existence.'

But Mississippi traffic did not stop when the war stopped.
The lesson had been learnt – heavy goods such as oil,
metal, grain, building materials, salt, sulphur, chemicals,
ores and scores of other products could be carried far more
economically by water than by land – and in some cases
almost as rapidly, thanks to the evolution of that marvel of
water transport, the diesel-powered towboat.

Ever since the war tonnage has increased year by year.
To take a single dramatic example, between 1946 and 1955
the Port of St Louis saw her river trade grow from 1,839,483
to 6,810,940 tons.

And yet the possible use of the river has only begun. There
is plenty of room left on the great highway. It is still a lonesome
river. You may sail it for hours without seeing another craft.

It is still a wayward and rebellious monster, only half-tamed.
Millions of dollars and thousands of men are constantly
working to improve its habits.

In view of the possibilities of better control, better boats,
perhaps atomic power, the Mississippi, already the most
heavily loaded river on this planet, may be only in the early
stages of its useful career.

2

Infant Mississippi

'YOU CAN GET pretty buggered up in there.'

That was a farmer's comment when we mentioned our plan to canoe down the first reach of the Mississippi River.

We did get pretty buggered up. In spite of the fact that I had the able assistance of two lusty lads, it was rough going. Fortunately the Grumman Aircraft aluminium canoe drew only three inches. It was thirteen feet long and weighed but forty-five pounds, therefore was light to carry around obstructions. But when you have almost nothing but obstructions for eighteen miles and repeatedly find yourself with a three-inch-draught boat in two inches of water, you are inclined to give this part of the river back to the mosquitoes.

We started out in high spirits. My wife had departed with the car to a point where the road crossed the river. There she would wait for us. Considering the wiggle of the little stream on the map, we estimated that the trip would take an hour.

It took five. We had scarcely left the lip of Lake Itasca when a disjointed old stone bridge, perhaps dating back to lumbering days, blocked our way. It was smothered in brush. We must pull the canoe out, beat a passage through the prickly brush, and carry around to the stream below the bridge.

We did repeat performances at four more bridges, all of them slumped too low to permit the canoe to pass under.

Even when the canoe was in the water we were seldom in the canoe. We were wading alongside, hauling or lifting the boat over pebbly shoals or rocky ledges. The shallows now and then gave way to deep holes, and we were soon soaked to the hips.

Then the forest fell back on both sides and the stream meandered through a great swamp a mile wide. We could stay in the boat now. The water was some twelve inches deep. But there was no discernible current to help our paddling.

At times there were several possible channels through the reeds and only the most learned debate could decide which we should take. My son, Bob, was a lawyer, therefore his arguments were not to be dismissed lightly. Jonathan was fifteen years old and had all the bright intuition and assurance of youth. I had the calm wisdom of maturity, not too much respected after I had steered the party up several culs-de-sac. Thus we whiled away the sunlit hours while Mary sat and waited.

* * *

The sinking sun found us still staggering about in the bewildering swamp. We were alone with our problem. There was no sign whatever that any other human beings inhabited the planet – no house, bridge or road, nothing but swamp a mile wide backed by forest.

The swamp had its own peculiar beauty. Brown cat-tails, blue iris, tawny reeds, yellow waterlilies were reflected in the sleeping water. Below us, what looked like pine forests in miniature rose almost to the surface, chambers of mystery like beds of coral.

The solitude was a lively solitude, ringing with song, for what could be a better bird paradise than this forest-bordered open swamp full of bugs and free of humans?

The red-winged blackbird's *gug-lug-gee* suggested perfectly the gurgle and ooze of the swamp. The purple grackle twanged his piano wires. The cedar waxwing gave a subdued imitation of a peanut-roaster's whistle. When we neared the trees we could hear the tinkling wine-glasses of the wood-thrush and the tremulous spiral of the veery who never seems quite able to make up his mind whether to play a Jew's-harp or an accordion.

Every few minutes a great blue heron cumbersomely took wing. Swallows dipped and soared. But the most common bird was one we had never seen before – black with grey wings edged in white. It swooped to within a few inches of our heads with a shrill *keek*. When later we had a chance to look it up in the bird book it proved to be the black tern. 'It migrates through the Mississippi valley and along coastal and salt marshes . . . and winters in South America.'

Muskrats and beavers swam out of our way. Deer stood at the edge of the woods. Woodland sounds were untranslatable, but we had already been told by the foresters that the animal population of this northernmost of all American states is still considerable.

The buffalo has vanished, but the majestic moose still roams the northern edge of the state, changing his nationality every few days as he crosses and recrosses the border. Moose are actually increasing in number.

The big grey timber-wolf, which we think of as belonging to the far past of the western pioneers or at least to the era of Jack London, is also increasing in the northern woods. In winter he ventures out on the ice of lakes and is hunted by plane for a bounty of $35.[1] A farmer's wife looked out of the window one day in 1957 to see a big timber-wolf trotting away through her garden with a lamb in its jaws. In the Wildlife Museum at Bemidji one may see a wolf that was killed within three miles of town.

It is said that the wolves are increasing because their

1. $1 is the approximate equivalent of 7s. 5d.

important food supply, the deer, are increasing. The bobcats also prey upon deer. They too are growing in number, not only because there are more deer available, but because the bounty of three dollars on bobcats is, with inflation, no longer an inducement to the trapper.

Not a few pet-loving farmers catch the deer while young and bring them up on the bottle. It is not unusual to see a domesticated deer wearing a collar and nosing about at the kitchen door of a farmhouse.

The grizzly is gone, but the black bear continues to be a source of amusement to visitors and distress to campers and rangers who have difficulty in guarding their food supplies. Bears will not hesitate to attack sheep. Turkey growers near Big Fork report heavy losses to bear and fox.

The bear's little cousin, the raccoon, delights visitors with its shrewd expression and mischievous antics but is considered one of the worst predators by farmers whose ducks it has slaughtered and whose nests it has robbed. In this land of lakes the raccoon does not need to go far to indulge its habit of washing its food before eating it. Should there be no water handy, the animal will go through the motions of washing the morsel, rubbing it vigorously between its hands.

We were to encounter skunks frequently in this wood-and-water country, and veteran trapper Henry Guertin of Deer River told us how to catch one: just seize it by the tail and lift it from the ground.

'The skunk can't spray unless it's gripping the ground with its front feet.'

We took his word for it and made no experiments.

*   *   *

The river had no interest in the shortest distance between two points. It looped back and forth upon itself, tripling and quadrupling the distance to our objective. We longed for a straight course and a fast one.

But when we got just that, we were far from satisfied. The river finally left the swamp, became straight and swift, and plunged down a chute several miles long between high banks supporting tall trees that met above to form a near-tunnel.

Though the river was now fast, we could not be, because the rapids were too shallow for navigation. We waded through the rocks, hoisting the canoe over the worst of them, stumbling into holes, feeling our way through the half-dark. Dusk had brought out the mosquitoes in millions. They eagerly lapped up the repellent we had spread on every inch of exposed skin. Every few dozen yards, a fallen tree blocked our way. We must carry around it through almost impenetrable under-brush.

And all this time we were going in the wrong direction. Wrong if we wished to reach New Orleans.

It was not our fault but that of the young and foolish Mississippi, which, ignorant of its destiny, was running hell-bent for the Arctic Ocean. For sixty miles the Mississippi flows north.

It takes its cue from the nearby Red River of the North which begins in the Itasca region and flows north across the border to Lake Winnipeg and Hudson Bay. Geologists tell us that the Missouri also flowed to Hudson Bay before the last Ice Age crossed its path with a glacier and diverted it to the Mississippi.

Following this prehistoric pattern the Mississippi sets out for Hudson Bay, but is blocked by a low ridge at Lake Bemidji. Being as yet a river of no great determination, it is easily persuaded to turn east. For some 120 miles the river very logically works its way towards Lake Superior. Again it has good precedent, for other rivers flow in the same direction and their waters reach the Great Lakes and ultimately the Atlantic Ocean. But when the young Mississippi is only about sixty miles from its goal it becomes discouraged and wanders irresolutely south.

The reason for this indecision is that northern Minnesota is a three-way watershed, spilling off to the north, east and south. This is the more remarkable since the roof of the watershed is relatively low. From Lake Itasca to the Gulf of Mexico the river drops only 1,475 feet. This means it is free to indulge in lazy meanderings, but it is a river of many moods and, after idly looping back and forth through many miles of slow gentle curves, it will suddenly hurl itself towards the Gulf with terrific resolution and devastating power.

North we went through the darkening tunnel. When we had begun to think of spending the night on a bed of leaves under a blanket of mosquitoes, the trees suddenly parted and there was the road bridge. The yellow car waited patiently and Mary a little less so. We flung the canoe on top of the car and drove to Bemidji State Park where our 21-foot travel trailer stood within a few yards of the north shore of Lake Bemidji.

3

Land of 10,000 Lakes

THE NEXT DAY we made the same trip but far more speedily and comfortably in Bob's little Navion. The river twisted like a tormented boa constrictor from Lake Itasca down to Lake Bemidji. In every direction were blue gems in dark settings. The Minnesota water-land in its far reaches is best seen from the air. Then you are quite willing to believe that it is the Land of Ten Thousand Lakes.

Minnesota is modest in this claim for, by official count, there are 11,007 lakes, not counting several thousand lakes and ponds of less than twenty-five acres.

How were these lakes formed? Actually by receding glaciers during the Ice Age. But a Minnesotan prefers to tell you that they were stamped out by the hooves of Paul Bunyan's giant Blue Ox.

And who was Paul Bunyan? The legend of this Hercules of the northwoods is said to have begun in the Papineau Rebellion in Canada in 1837 when a 'mighty-muscled, bellicose, bearded giant named Paul Bunyan ... raged among the Queen's troops like Samson among the Philistines'. The Scandinavians who swarmed into Minnesota during lumbering days adopted the giant, perhaps because he reminded them of their mythical Thor. At any rate, lumberjacks were physically a superior breed of men and loved to tell of feats of great strength in the battle with the big trees. And so, not only in these woods but in the timber country from Maine to Oregon, big and humour-loving men took delight in spinning yarns about the biggest of them all, Paul Bunyan.

On the Bemidji lakefront a log-building houses an amusing collection of articles supposed once to have belonged to the redoubtable Paul – a gigantic axe, a pair of gloves five feet long, dice a foot high, a gun as big as a cannon, a watch with a chain strong enough to moor an ocean liner. Outside on the shore stand two sky-reaching statues of Paul and his ox.

The town of Bemidji once had fourteen sawmills and cut a million feet of lumber a day. Scratch the ground and you still find sawdust. The stories have it that it was in this busy lumber town that Paul Bunyan first saw the light. It took five storks to deliver him to his parents.

It is not stated whether the same storks brought Babe, the Blue Ox, who grew to be so big that the camp laundryman hung out the wash on his horns.

One day the camp tankwagon which Babe hauled sprang a leak. This created Lake Itasca and the overflow made the Mississippi River.

Babe had a good appetite. He would eat fifty bales of hay for dinner, wire and all. Then he would settle back and let six men with picaroons pick the wire out of his teeth.

Babe had to have a watering trough and that was why Paul, in an odd moment, dug out Lake Superior.

Paul was a typical lumberjack, but on a large scale. He towered above the tallest trees and his stride covered twenty-four townships. His slightest whisper would make a cyclone in the Caribbean and he could let out a bellow that would cause a landslide on Pike's Peak. Every time he sneezed he blew the roof off the bunkhouse and his speaking voice made it necessary for his lumberjacks to wear earmuffs the year round.

All lumberjacks were great men in those days. Paul's cook, Sourdough Sam, used a griddle covering about an acre, and his hundred helpers greased it by skating over it with slabs of bacon strapped to their feet. When the straw boss sent some logs to New Orleans by mistake he brought them back by sucking up the Mississippi. The camp bookkeeper, Johnny Inkslinger, seems to have been the inventor of the fountain-pen. By means of a hose he connected his pen with a barrel of ink and saved five barrels a year by not dotting his i's and crossing his t's.

* * *

Where the river gives up its Arctic ambitions and turns east, it flows out of Lake Bemidji in a noble stream two hundred feet wide, contrasting strongly with the ten-foot rivulet in the first reaches.

The river is now navigable for small craft. No longer need we carry the canoe – it will carry us. So begins a 400-mile canoe trip down one of the most delightful of rivers. The journey is pretty soft compared to those of the early *voyageurs*. We do not camp out. At the end of the day's stint we find the car waiting for us and drive back to spend the night in our mobile home.

This means there must be a driver to bring the car. After the boys have flown home to Massachusetts, a visiting sister takes over for a few days and thereafter we must find someone, perhaps at a garage, to perform this service.

The day's routine is simple, at least in theory. Our helper huddles with us over a map to decide where he shall meet us. It should be a point about twenty-five miles downstream. That is an easy day's paddle, allowing time for picture-taking, lunch, inquisitive side-trips, perhaps a portage or two. Our driver is to have the car at the meeting point at 5 p.m. Having fortified ourselves with a good breakfast, Mary and I embark. The trip that takes us all day takes our driver half an hour. At 4.30 he steps into the car, drives it down to the rendezvous, picks us up and we return to our trailer. Every few days the trailer is moved another hundred miles downstream.

On the whole, it works well. But there are a few things that can happen, and do.

The driver forgets, or happens to be busy at 4.30. Or the point of meeting has been misunderstood. He waits at one spot, we wait at another. He concludes that we have been picked up by someone else and goes home. We spend the night on pine needles under the canoe.

Or we have been dumped in the rapids. Wet and shivering in a cold wind, we would much rather go back to headquarters at once than wait until late afternoon. If there is a farmhouse and a telephone handy, we are in luck. But there is more likely to be solid forest flanking the river on both sides. We must wring ourselves out as best we can and go on.

But, barring accidents, the plan provides one great luxury that the explorers never knew: home at the end of the day. The modern trailer is a model of convenience and comfort, and takes most of the travail out of travel.

The Mississippi is a secretive river. It is almost unknown to many people who live within a few miles of it. Over some stretches the road hugs the shore and magnificent views may be had of the river and its maze of islands. But for the most part the highway does not attempt to follow the river's meanderings. You may drive from the Canadian border to the Gulf following the general route of the Mississippi and scarcely be aware of its existence. If you are determined, you can reach it by small side-roads, often unpaved. And, of course, it can be seen from the bridges.

But by far the best way to see the Mississippi is over the bow of your own boat. Lacking the inclination to take your own, you may hire boats, motored or motorless, at many points along the river.

*   *   *

It is easy to imagine oneself a Joliet or Marquette while paddling down this undiscovered river. It flows today as it flowed then between unbroken walls of dark green conifers and snow-white birch. It slows in lilied swamps or speeds down narrow chutes between threatening boulders. It embraces charming islands and swirls rudely around rocky capes.

It is clear and pure for hundreds of miles before its confluence with the turbid Missouri, and when it pauses long enough to smooth the wrinkles from its forehead its clean surface reflects the flight of kingfishers and herons and black terns. You may paddle for half a day without sight of a bridge or a house or a human. It is your river, for your boat alone. If after long hours of solitude you see another boat, you are surprised and a little indignant.

Minnesota has more than its share of the Mississippi. The river runs a third of its total course before it leaves the state. This is the most beautiful third of the river. The other two thirds deserve another adjective, perhaps 'majestic'.

Seeking variety, the young Mississippi frequently broadens into a lake. After Lake Bemidji come Wolf and Andrusia, then unique Cass Lake with its island enclosing another lake – a jewel within a jewel. Cass became notable for its house-to-house mail delivery by water, the mail being picked up by a launch from boxes set well out into the lake.

Much larger is Winnebigoshish. The name means 'Miserable, wretched, dirty water', stemming from the fact that the lake is so shallow that storms easily disturb it and turn up extremely dangerous choppy waves.

Ball Club Lake does not owe its name to baseball. Its namer thought that it was shaped like a lacrosse racquet.

What a colossal task it must have been to name all of Minnesota's 11,007 lakes is evident in the names themselves. The Indian names, where they existed, were usually too difficult for the settlers from Europe. A few of the newcomers picked poetic names: Sylvan, Alpine, Elysian and the like.

But the average pioneer was not poetic. He was content with such names as Kettle, Spider, Spoon, Pickle, Plum, Duck, Turtle, Rum, and Whisky.

Some incident or adventure may have prompted Big Spunk, Split Hand, Little Dead Horse, Full of Fish, and Dirty Nose.

Scandinavians immortalized their own names in Big Ole, Peterson, Olson, Swede, and Kolstad; and the Irish adorned the map with Kelly, Murphy, O'Leary, and O'Brien.

Many men thought alike and there are more than a hundred Long Lakes, scores of Rices and several dozen Muds.

When imagination failed completely lakes were dubbed One, Two, Three, Four, Five, Six, etc., and others suffer under the names First, Second, Third.

It is astonishing that no one seems to have thought of the letters of the alphabet. Here is a gold-mine still to be tapped, should new lakes appear.

However, geologists predict that the number of lakes will not increase, but decrease. Reeds and weeds, bulrushes and cattails, waterlilies and many sorts of aquatic plants gradually crowd out the water. The lake becomes a swamp, the swamp becomes a wet prairie, and the wet prairie is drained, naturally or artificially, and becomes a farm. But it is a slow process, and for some centuries yet Minnesota may safely claim to be the Land of Ten Thousand Lakes.

King of all swimming things in this fish paradise is the mighty muskellunge. At Leech Lake, which flows to the Mississippi, we found the battle with the giants in full swing. Muskies measure up to eight feet and may weigh more than one hundred pounds. They are carnivores and cannibals and like nothing better than a fight. They lurk in the shallows behind a rock and dart out with incredible speed to catch a fish, a frog or a muskrat or leap from the water to snap up a low-flying bird. If there is nothing else to eat they do not hesitate to devour each other.

Trolling for muskies is exciting. The fish leaps from the water and attacks the lure so savagely that he sometimes breaks off a few teeth. Once hooked, he does not give up easily. He shoots up from the water and tosses his head back and forth like a dog, trying to shake himself free. When at last hauled in he is still full of fury and the prospect of sharing a boat with a thrashing fish as long as a man is not inviting. It takes a blow that would stun an ox to put him out of business, and many an apparently dead muskie has revived long enough to smash a boat's fittings and break a fisherman's arm or leg.

*   *   *

In the quieter stretches of the river the canoe slid through reedy shallows that reminded us of the water-soaked rice fields of Japan. Arriving in Grand Rapids (Minnesota) we enquired about what we had seen.

Yes, it had been rice, but wild – a commodity in which Minnesota does a million dollars worth of business a year. At the storehouse of the Arrowhead Wild Rice Company we were told the story of wild rice.

It grows in shallow lakes and in the quiet backwaters of the Mississippi. It has always been one of the staple foods of the Indians. They still rely upon it, therefore the government protects it and places restrictions upon harvesting. The boat used by harvesters must not be more than thirty inches wide and sixteen feet long so that it will not destroy too much grain in passing. No motors are allowed. The flail (a sort of club) must not be more than thirty inches long. The heads are bent over the boat and struck with the flail so that the ripe grain falls into the boat. Heavy flails or mechanical harvesters would destroy the unripe kernels. If not destroyed, these can be harvested later, at intervals.

The hours of harvesting are from eight in the morning until six in the evening. The non-Indians must have a licence –

one dollar for the season. The dealer's licence is $75. Game wardens are constantly on the prowl during the harvesting month, September, and strictly enforce these regulations.

The squaw sits in the middle of the boat, bending the rice inward and knocking off the kernels. Her buck stands at the stern and propels the boat with a long forked pole. It is the old way, and white harvesters must use the same method.

There is money in wild rice. Some boats make forty to eighty dollars a day.

'An Indian girl,' said our informer, 'begged off from her job as a domestic servant for a few days because she said her doctor had ordered her to rest. Her real reason was that she wanted to harvest wild rice. It was a far heavier job than domestic service, but she could make fifty dollars a day at it. I think the record was chalked up last season by one boat [two men] harvesting a thousand pounds a day at forty cents a pound, a take of four hundred dollars a day. But they were experts.'

Wild rice is parched like coffee, threshed to remove the husks, air-cleaned and polished. Then it is packaged and put on the market. The price is fairly high but justified by the expense of harvesting and processing. Among many delightful wild rice dishes are Wild Rice and Mushrooms, Spanish Wild Rice, Stuffing for Wild Game and Fish, Wild Rice Curry, Baked Steak Stuffed with Wild Rice, Wild Rice Breakfast Cakes, and a royal concoction of pork, ham, sausage, onions, bay leaf, parsley and wild rice known as Wild Rice Jambalaya.

*　　*　　*

A pow-wow sounds like fun. The word suggests a hilarious party. Yet there was something infinitely melancholy about the Chippewa pow-wow we witnessed in the depths of the

Minnesota forest. To the beat of drums sad-faced men, women and children circled about in what was supposed to be a dance but was little more than a walk.

As the beer intake increased, the clouds lifted sufficiently to allow for a few songs. The Chippewas find escape and relief in music. When an Indian comes back from a visit to another reservation he is immediately asked, 'What new songs did you learn?'

There are dream songs, hunting songs, love-charm songs, healing songs, songs praying for a good supply of maple sugar, songs of battle and death. There are songs that recall the exile of the Chippewas from their homeland. These are the more simple and poignant because they are not sprinkled with any self-pitying adjectives:

'Come
It is time to depart
We are going a long journey'.

The whites always paid for the land they took, but often with only food, liquor and trickery. The entire upper half of what is now the State of Minnesota was ceded away by the Chippewas. The immediate benefits they got in exchange satisfied most Indians, but one chief who could see farther than the others considered the price too low, saying, 'You forget that the land will be yours as long as the world lasts.'

The white man's diseases contributed to the decimation of the tribes. An incident still remembered and enshrined in song is the smallpox epidemic of 1837.

A steamboat of the American Fur Company came up into the Indian country with several cases of smallpox on board. At a river port the Indians, despite warnings, insisted upon going on board and one made off with a blanket infected with the smallpox virus. Very soon several Indians were down with the dread disease.

The commander of the fur company's fort decided to vaccinate all the Indians in the district. He drew the vaccine from the existing smallpox cases, not realizing it was much too powerful to be administered to Indians with no racial immunity to smallpox. Of thirty squaws he vaccinated, twenty-seven promptly came down with the disease in its most malignant form, many of them dying within twenty-four hours. The survivors fled in every direction, spreading the disease far and wide. Before the epidemic ran its course it killed seventeen thousand of the Blackfeet, Assiniboins, Mandans, Arikaras, Crows and Sioux. An eyewitness reported,

'The atmosphere, for miles, is poisoned by the stench of hundreds of carcasses unburied. The women and children are wandering in groups without food, or howling over the dead. The men are flying in every direction. The proud, warlike, and noble-looking Blackfeet are no more. Their deserted lodges are seen on every hill. The desolation is appalling – beyond the imagination to conceive.'

More effectively than many battles, the epidemic destroyed Indian resistance. It was germ warfare a century before its time, differing from the modern version only in that it was unintentional.

The American Indians are not a dying race. In spite of all their adversities, they steadily increase in number. They are, however, a disappearing race, becoming steadily less noticeable because of the rapid growth of the white population. They leave few enduring monuments. Their wigwams and log-cabins have crumbled to dust, their camp-sites are overgrown, their houses and shacks in the reservations are like the homes of many of their white neighbours.

It is a curious anomaly that the Indians are leaving less to remember them by than has been left by their predecessors. Up and down the Mississippi Valley and elsewhere in the country stand some ten thousand earthen pyramids, artificial hills rising three to five storeys tall. They are believed to have been built by aborigines who antedated the Indian tribes. Particularly near Greenville, Mississippi, the Winterville Mounds constitute what archaeologists have called 'the most spectacular display of earthworks on the North American continent'. This group consists of a large central mound surrounded by fourteen others in an irregular ellipse. Why they were built is not clear, but they seem to have had religious significance and seem also to have been used as forts and tombs.

Their builders appear to have been more highly civilized than the Indians who came later. The hunting and household implements that have been dug up, the pottery vessels, the copper tools, the arrows, fishhooks, beads, pipes, are superior to most Indian artifacts.

A fossil skeleton known as 'Minnesota Man' and judged to be twenty thousand years old is more definitely Mongoloid than the Indian or Eskimo, long-headed instead of round-headed. The 'Browns Valley Man', whose age is estimated at twelve thousand years, had features quite different from those of the modern Indian. The mounds, however, are not judged to be extremely old and it may have been less than a thousand years ago that their civilized builders disappeared, perhaps exterminated or absorbed by the incoming Indians. It would not be the first time that a higher civilization has been wiped out by a lower. That story has been repeated many times since the savage Gauls and Huns sacked Rome.

4

The Parboiled Nudes

AT ONE OF THE RARE waterside farms we saw on the beach a small square cabin belching both smoke and steam from its chimneys. Could this be a Finnish *sauna*?

We disembarked and examined the cubicle. It was almost as windowless as a fort and the door was closed. We walked up to the farmhouse. From a radio inside the house came talk in a strange language, then song, equally strange. It was certainly not German nor Scandinavian.

Our knock brought a big, cheerful rosy-faced man to the door. He spoke English without accent, yet he had been listening to a foreign-language programme. He welcomed us in, then turned off the radio.

'Was that a Finnish programme?' I asked.

'That's right. They call it the Finnish Hour.'

'But can you understand it? You weren't born in Finland.'

'No, I was born right here. But my parents and grandparents spoke Finnish, so of course I picked it up. There are plenty of Finns in Minnesota, you know. And a lot of them still speak Finnish.'

'And take their baths Finnish style?'

'Oh, you saw the *sauna*. Yes, that's one Finnish custom we won't give up. I suppose you've seen how it works.'

We confessed that we had not. He took us down to the cubicle on the beach. A girl, completely nude, was just coming out of the door. Her whole body radiated steam as if she were walking in a mist. Quite undisturbed by our presence, she ran across the beach and plunged into the water.

We went inside. First there was a small dressing-room. Beyond it was the steam room fitted with a bench where the whole family and perhaps a few guests could sit, soap themselves and swelter in the steam. To increase the effect, they might beat each other with switches of prickly oak leaves, or birch twigs. When they could bear no more, they would run out and dive into the river.

Across from the bench was a wood stove. On top of it was a huge pan filled with rocks. The rocks gave off tremendous heat. But there was no sign of a boiler or other steam-producing equipment.

'How do you make the steam?'

'I'll show you.' He took up a wooden bucket, filled it from a large tub, and threw the water over the stones. The water fell on the hot rocks with a noise like machine-gun fire. A dense cloud of hot steam immediately filled the little room. We choked, and backed out.

But the proud Finn would not be satisfied until at least one of us had tried it. With grave doubts, I disrobed in the dressing-room, went into the steam room and closed the door. The fire was burning briskly and the stones glowed. Sitting on the bench, I found myself already dripping wet, thanks to the humidity.

After soaping myself, I flung a bucketful of water on the stones. The sudden steam made me gasp for breath. More and more water went on the stones, and more and more I progressed towards a state of complete suffocation.

Perspiration streamed out of me like juice from a squeezed orange. In ten minutes I felt as wrung out as a rag. For five years in Japan I had taken a daily bath in water three feet deep, heated to one hundred and twenty degrees, but it was nothing like this. The steam went up the nostrils and down into the lungs and I felt baked from both the inside and the outside. My head seemed about to explode.

'Out already?' said my Finnish host as I burst through the door and ran to plunge my stewing body in the river. Later the ceremony was completed with a mug of mulled cider in the farmhouse. Now I was feeling the afterglow. It was like sinking into a featherbed a mile deep. Every muscle, every nerve, was relaxed. A shoulder that had become paddle-lame was now perfectly at ease.

'It's good for neuralgia,' said the farmer's wife. 'And colds.'

'You take these baths in winter too?'

'Certainly.'

'But then you can't go in the river. It must be frozen over.'

'Yes. We roll in the snow instead. A drift six feet deep forms against the north wall of the *sauna*. We have great fun in it.'

As in Japan, the two sexes bathe together in the nude and take their cooling-off together in the water or the snow. A boy may come to see his girl and bathe with her and her family. And yet at other times strict propriety is observed. At the bathing beaches, even though swimming suits are worn, it is Finnish custom for men and women to bathe separately.

The difference lies in the fact that the bath in the *sauna* is not just a bath. Traditionally it is a ceremony.

'The bathhouse is a kind of temple,' writes Arthur Reade in *Finland and the Finns*, 'and the bath has the nature of a ritual. The church and the bathhouse are holy places, says a Finnish proverb. The place has grave and lofty associations of another kind also. It is to the bathhouse that the mother retires when a child is about to be born and the temperature is made as high as possible in order to ease her delivery. To it also sick people are taken as to a hospital.'

*   *   *

There's a long carry at Grand Rapids. A dam has taken the

place of the rapids that gave the town its name, and above the dam the river is surfaced with several acres of logs waiting to be ground into pulp and turned into paper in the mill of the Blandin Paper Company.

This is one of the longest of the fourteen carries around dams on the way to Minneapolis. There navigation for large craft begins and every dam is supplemented by a lock. From Minneapolis to the Gulf, one need never take one's craft out of the water.

The logs awaiting pulverization remind us that lumbering is not yet dead on the Mississippi. To be sure, the logs are rarely floated down-river as they once were, but go by truck and train. Six million acres of commercial forest lie within easy reach of Grand Rapids. The days of wholesale slaughter are gone. Now cutting does not keep up with growth. Forest surveys show that only a half to two-thirds of the allowable cut each year is harvested.

The foresters develop new stands and protect old ones. The paper mill, when it buys logs from tree farms, gives the farmer seedlings to grow new trees. So the supply is maintained. There is a shortage of some trees, but spruce (valuable for paper) is increasing and 'there's more poplar than we know what to do with'.

Not only is the Blandin mill dependent upon the Mississippi for power, but great quantities of water are required in paper making. And the water must be pure. Most important, it must oe free of iron, which turns paper brown. The Mississippi meets these exacting requirements. (The same could not be said of it a thousand miles later.)

That the river should be untouched by iron is the more remarkable since it skirts one of the greatest iron reserves in the world, the famous Mesabi Range. Great open pits sometimes miles wide and hundreds of feet deep yawn like smaller Grand Canyons or volcanic craters, and men and machinery at work far below are reduced to the size of toys. As the supply diminishes, the demand for more iron grows and activity in the pits becomes more feverish. Mining employment in Minnesota increased ninety-nine per cent from 1940 to 1950 as against nineteen per cent in the U.S. as a whole. Two-thirds of the nation's iron ore comes from the Minnesota pits.

5

Lumberjacks and Monsters

IN THIS LAND with its traditions of lumbermen as big as trees and man-made canyons it is not surprising to hear that the waters are inhabited by a monster.

It was first reported by lumberjacks some sixty years ago. They claimed to have seen it in McKinney Lake, just north of the village of Grand Rapids. The villagers flocked to the lake and, sure enough, there in plain sight was an enormous snakelike creature fifty or sixty feet long, writhing angrily in the waves and rolling great white eyes at the tasty human morsels on the shore. Many fled back to the safety of the village. The more daring fired guns at the monster which did not seem to mind the peppering in the least.

As time passed and the creature did not stir from its position in the lake, men grew bolder. Finally two leading citizens screwed up their courage to pay the monster a visit. They made their wills, bade farewell to their loved ones, and set out in a rowboat. As they approached their objective it looked less and less like a sea-serpent and more like a string of beer kegs fastened together by the chains that were used in tying together log rafts. Wind and waves gave the string of kegs a serpentine movement. The head was a carved pine root and two white billiard balls attached to it looked like staring eyes. It was a joke characteristic of the lumberjacks, big men who must do everything in a big way.

Brawny Norwegians, Swedes and Finns, wiry Scots, Irishmen and French Canadians, staunch Germans, Poles and Lithuanians, made their own United Nations in the timber country. A dozen languages were heard in the lumber towns and the only common speech was the timber slang. Everybody knew that a turkey was the lumberman's dufflebag, a nosebag carried his cold lunch, hay was his pay, logging berries were prunes, a skypiece was a hat, a gazabo was any worker, a deacon seat was a bench in the bunkhouse, a groundhog was the man who pried the logs out of the dirt with his peavy, and to get your stem cracked meant to break your leg.

'Tumble out!' started the day, and 'Breakfast on the boards!' meant vast quantities of pancakes, hash and beans devoured at breakneck speed. By dawn the great crosscuts were already bringing down trees and by noon there could be twenty thousand feet of logs sliding down to the river over roads iced during the night by road monkeys driving tank sprinklers.

At noon the men did not go to camp. The camp came to them. The bull cook drove out over the tote road into the woods in a box sled full of kettles of hot food. His dinner horn could be heard for miles and his 'It's goin' to waste!' brought the men in droves.

At night they swarmed into camp, sat down at the long tables in the cookhouse and reached for platters of hot meat, mashed potatoes, pancakes, beans, bread, rolls and biscuits, apple pies, rice puddings, and there was no one to say 'Hold, enough!' One company's annual bill for groceries might easily top $250,000. It was company policy to feed the men well so they could work well. Said one newcomer, 'This one bully country, every day Christmas.' Men who came into the woods lean and hungry went out in the spring fat and sassy.

The horses fared equally well. The teamster was devoted to his team and saw to it that they lacked nothing. One

Scandinavian driver even shared his chewing tobacco with
his animals. The moment he drew his plug from his pocket
his horses began to whinny and were not satisfied until there
was none left. 'Dose damn horses,' he complained, 'keep me
broke buyin' 'em chewin' tobacco.'

*　　*　　*

An interesting survival or revival of lumbering days is to
be found on Gull Lake near Brainerd. Here two historically-
minded resort owners, Jack and Peg Madden, have created
Lumbertown. It is an authentic replica of a Minnesota
lumber town of the 1870s. On the three streets stand fourteen old-time buildings, and at least seven more are to be
added.

You feel that you have stepped back a century as you stroll
down the plank sidewalk past the old red schoolhouse, the
log-built pioneer home, the ice cream parlour, the photographer's shop, the cobbler's bench, the fire barn and the
blacksmith's shop to the Headquarters Hotel which, like its
predecessor of the same name in Brainerd, serves family-style
chicken and wall-eyed pike dinners with blueberry pie by
the light of kerosene lamps.

Passing the harness shop and the livery barn you cross Dead
Man's Gulch to the tonsorial and dental parlour, the general
store, the art museum and the sunbonnet shop.

In front of the Last Turn Saloon the boardwalk is built
around a pine tree as a reminder of the Norway pine which
once stood before this hotel in Brainerd. On one of its branches
two Indians were hanged in a hurry, only to be found
innocent soon after.

The general store is stocked with the goods of the last
century and the pioneer home not only has the old furnishings
but the old lady who lived in this house as a girl. Mrs Van
Sickle takes delight in showing how housekeeping was done

in a square-hewn log cabin. In the schoolhouse that stands next door she was one of the pupils and later served as teacher.

Everything is as authentic as careful research can make it. The pioneer home and red schoolhouse were brought from Pillager, so named from the tribe of Indians who killed Chippewa Chief Hole-in-the-Day. The general store was brought in bodily from Aitkin. Many of the other buildings are actual transplants, and the rest are faithful replicas.

The lumberjacks and girls who stroll the streets and serve in the shops and hotel are not a century old, but their costumes made before the turn of the century make it easy to believe that they belong to a day gone by.

Brainerd vies with Bemidji in claiming Paul Bunyan as a past resident. An animated figure of the famous lumberjack with 150-inch waist and 80-inch neck towers 23 feet high, moves his arms and eyes, and in a deep voice that seems to issue from his mouth tells stories to visiting children. He is surrounded by buildings and implements of logging days – a logging camp containing bunkhouse and cook shack, the great wheels used to haul out tall timber, and a sled to carry water for icing the roads so that log sleds could pass over them more easily. The icing sled is equipped with a built-in stove to keep the water from freezing before it could be applied to the roads.

* * *

In the marvellous lake country above Brainerd the Mississippi runs between high banks and the stream is too swift for frogs or wild rice. White rapids tumble over unseen rocks. We slide along with toboggan speed. The current is full of whirlpools with doughnut-holes in their centres – but though they sometimes twist the boat out of control for a moment they are never powerful enough to upend it and suck it down as the whirls in the lower river sometimes swallow logs.

Great blue herons and kingfishers sail from one forest wall across to the other. Deer come down to the shore to drink. If deer-flies are any indication of the presence of deer there must be great herds in these woods.

The deer-flies sail round and round our heads and we have to be continually dropping our paddles to swat them. Our conversation is punctuated with impolite exclamations, the whang of dropped paddles, and resounding slaps on tortured skins.

Repellent seems to have no effect, unless it actually attracts the flies. They calmly sit in puddles of the stuff and proceed to bite. We seek reassurance by reading the label on the bottle. It shows beautiful pictures of flies, but the text mentions only black-flies, sand-flies, stable-flies, not deer-flies.

The regional distribution of insects is curious and hard to understand. We had had no deer-flies on other stretches of the river, only mosquitoes. Here there is not a single mosquito, but clouds of deer-flies.

They are stupid as well as vicious. They get tangled up in one's hair, blunder into ears, eyes and mouth. But they do not lack talent when they bite.

*   *   *

Then we come to a more peaceful part of the river, free of deer-flies, and temporarily desert our canoe in favour of a houseboat. It is the *Mary Ann* owned by E. M. Leckband of Snug Harbor, and this is its maiden voyage.

We have interesting companions: a veteran authority on the river, the secretary of the Brainerd Chamber of Commerce, officers of the Minnesota Historical Society, an archaeologist, a judge, and the Indian Agent.

The craft is a two-decker, the upper deck uncovered so that the view on all sides and above is unhindered. The lower deck is also pleasant, screened but not glassed. There is a small cooking stove, some dishes, a long table, plenty of chairs, a wheel up forward, a 25-horsepower outboard motor aft.

The boat, fully loaded, draws only five inches. It proceeds almost noiselessly and with a minimum of vibration. It is pleasant, for a change, to proceed under power other than our own. The view from the upper deck over the mirror-smooth river is enchanting.

From now on we are to see and sample many houseboats, and certainly no more delightful river craft can be imagined than these homes afloat. They range from the simplest home-made contraptions to floating palaces costing tens of thousands of dollars.

6

Small Boat, Big River

PERHAPS our idle idyll by houseboat made us soft. At any rate when we went back to our paddles we found ourselves faced with the hardest job in all our canoe experience.

It looked so easy. The current was strong and we expected it to carry us along with little or no effort on our part.

But a violent headwind developed. Many travellers down the Mississippi have complained of the prevailing south wind. Generally it is only a breeze; this time it grew into a gale.

It was like trying to paddle through a stone wall. The opposition was so strong that if we stopped paddling for an instant the wind promptly blew us upstream against the current. The blasts all but whipped the paddles out of our hands. Many times we ran into sea-size waves as the result of upstream wind against downstream current. They showered over us and nearly swamped the boat. The river was in places a half mile wide – much too wide for comfort in a strong wind. A helicopter from nearby Camp Ripley returned time and again to see if we were still above water.

Whenever the wind battering our eyeballs would let us, we realized that the river was beautiful. Hundreds of islands lay between the low shore on the right and the high rugged bank on the left. Deer looked out from the island woods. It is said that they take refuge there because the mainland has become too busy – though we went many miles without seeing a house.

But it was often difficult to pick the most direct channel through the islands. At one place there were five broad passages to confuse us.

We ran into rapids repeatedly, nine times within one period of six hours and the rapids were full of ugly rocks.

The wind and waves were so noisy that, sitting only ten feet apart, we could not hear each other speak. The waves curled and broke over us, the surface was churned into white-caps and we seemed to be afloat on a sea of whipped cream.

We were quite willing to give up the struggle. But then what? A night on an island, the wind chilling us through our wet clothes? If we could just find a house, we could telephone. There was no house. Even the helicopter had deserted us.

It got worse when the river began to broaden into a lake at Little Falls. The lake was one roaring rush of water, the wind dead against us. But there at last was a small pier. We pulled in behind it, walked half a mile back through the woods until we came upon a farmhouse and telephoned our driver to come and pick us up. It was the first time we had fallen short of our objective, but we acknowledged defeat with the greatest pleasure.

* * *

Glass, which is transforming modern architecture, performs another miracle at Little Falls. It makes boats.

'We were forced out of the manufacture of wooden boats,' said Lem Larson, builder of glass boats, 'by the labour cost. It's a long process. It took us two weeks to make a wooden boat. But if we get an order for a custom-made fibreglass boat Monday morning we can deliver it Wednesday evening. Three days against fourteen.'

'But how does the fibreglass boat stand up compared with a wooden or aluminium boat?'

'A lot better. It has the advantage that it can be easily

moulded to any shape. The colour is in the material. Doesn't need to be laid on, never needs to be renewed. A fibreglass boat doesn't need to be reconditioned at the beginning of the season, as other boats do.'

'But isn't the stuff brittle?'

Lem picked up a slab of fibreglass plastic composition an eighth of an inch thick. He beat on it with a hammer. The blows had no effect upon the slab.

'Wood wouldn't stand that. Do it to a metal boat and you'd have a hole, or at least a bad dent. The plastic alone wouldn't stand it. It's the fibreglass that holds it together.'

From Little Falls on for almost a thousand miles the Mississippi is the ideal home of small boats. But after the Missouri and the Ohio swell its stream, Old Man River becomes too strong, sullen and treacherous for small craft. However, a few canoe trips have been made all the way to the Gulf, and there are always backwaters and bayous where local residents can fish and sail in safety.

* * *

About St Cloud yawn the quarries that make this area the world's largest producer of coloured granite. When you come to rest under a tombstone the chances are it will be of St Cloud granite. Your name and an appropriate sentiment in your honour will have been carved upon it, not by an engraver's tool, but by the sand-blast method.

We saw it done in a St Cloud monument plant. The design and lettering were first traced on a rubber blanket. This was laid over the stone and the pattern was cut out wherever the stone was to be engraved. Then a sand-blast machine poured out a stream of sharp particles of abrasive materials under high pressure to carve the lettering deep into the granite. Angels, cherubs, wreathes and what-not were sandblasted into the stone by the same method.

Equally remarkable were the machines that received huge blocks of granite and sliced them into thin slabs as if they were cheese. The slicing is done by a stream of shot, the sort that is used by a boy in his first gun. The shot is delivered by an overhead water stream and dragged over the stone by a moving wire. The oldtime gravestone maker who did everything by hand would be quite bewildered among the smarter-than-human machines of a St Cloud monument plant.

St Cloud granite, coming in many different colours, surfaces with enduring beauty thousands of buildings in America and overseas.

7

The Heavenly Twins

THE CANOEIST PADDLES through much of Minneapolis
scarcely aware that the city exists. In the heart of Minnesota's
greatest metropolitan area the river still struggles to maintain
its privacy. It passes through a sylvan canyon closed in on
both sides by wooded banks some hundred feet high.

The gorge is a quiet bird sanctuary and probably about as
it was when man first saw it, except that it is now crossed by
bridges. These are so high above that they hardly disturb
travellers on the river. For long stretches no houses are to be
seen, yet we find later when we drive along the river roads that
only a screen of trees shuts off beautiful residential districts
from the solitude-loving river.

An unimportant-looking little stream comes in from the
right, but this trivial trickle is one of the most loved waters in
America. It is Minnehaha Creek, immortalized by Longfellow.

After skirting Lake Harriet which with Lake Calhoun,
Cedar Lake, Lake of the Isles and many other exquisite
sheets of water give Minneapolis the name City of Lakes, the
woodland creek touches Lake Nokomis, passes through Lake
Hiawatha, divides to embrace the island on which stands the
bronze of Hiawatha about to bear his sweetheart across the
stream.

'Over wide and rushing rivers
In his arms he bore the maiden;
Light he thought her as a feather,
As the plume upon his head-gear.'

Then the stream plunges over the precipice to the delight of daily thousands of admiring visitors.

'Where the Falls of Minnehaha
Flash and gleam among the oak trees,
Laugh and leap into the valley.'

A little after the advent of the famous creek, we pass under old Fort Snelling, for more than thirty years the northernmost post of the U.S. Army. Here the Minnesota River quietly joins the Mississippi.

As if this reinforcement gave the river the courage to face the world, the Mississippi now flows through the busiest part of St Paul fully exposed to view and affording docking facilities for large river craft.

So far as commercial traffic is concerned, the Mississippi begins at the Twin Cities. There the Falls of St Anthony block off the upper reaches. This is most inconvenient for Minneapolis whose chief industrial district lies above the Falls.

To tap this industrial area, the Falls are now to be by-passed by two great locks. The lower lock, already built, has a lift of twenty-five feet. The upper lock, planned for completion in 1962, will hoist boats fifty feet, the highest lift on the entire Mississippi. The present champion is Keokuk Lock with a lift of 38·2 feet.

Above the locks an 'Upper Harbor' 4·6 miles long will be constructed, comparable to the Port of New Orleans, and serving in this case a metropolitan area of one and a half million people.

* * *

We parked our trailer on the shore of pretty Tanner Lake on the eastern outskirts of St Paul. From a small Cessna plane we got an overall view of the Twins with their lovely tree-sheltered streets, many parks, gleaming lakes, the Mississippi winding through in a great S.

Entering the concourse of St Paul's City Hall, we paid our respects to the sixty-ton Indian three storeys tall, the largest carved onyx figure in the world, the work of the Swedish sculptor Carl Milles. To show the details on the back of the figure, it revolves slowly on a turntable base, completing a ninety-degree arc every hour.

We went upstairs to see Mayor Joseph E. Dillon, a very young man yet quite obviously not a member of the 'beat generation'. He is the thoughtful type and speaks with quiet authority. He is fond of the river and, as a boating enthusiast, knows it well.

He walked with us a few blocks to the First National Bank Building, St Paul's highest, and from its roof pointed out a large area in a bend of the Mississippi across from the business centre of St Paul. There was little to be seen but swamp, trees and some shacks.

'It doesn't look like much now,' he said. 'It's been flooded twice in recent years. Naturally industry is afraid to build there. But we have great plans for it. The engineers are going to dike it in so there'll be no more flooding. Then we hope to reclaim about three thousand acres and bring in industries. Not just any industries but industries that can use the river.

'We aren't realizing at present the potential value of the Mississippi. It is America's great north-south axis. The trouble with us is that we think east-westwise, not north-south. We buy and sell with New York, Chicago, San Francisco, but we ignore the great opportunities that are opening up in the southern states.

'The Mississippi offers us direct communication with the south. Nothing else does. No single airline runs south to the

Gulf. To go there you would probably fly to Chicago or St Louis, then take another plane to New Orleans. No one railroad will carry you through from here to New Orleans. Our great railroads run east and west. The Mississippi is a road to the south and we should use it more than we do.'

*　　*　　*

Some strange things go on in St Paul. A proportion of the inhabitants are cave dwellers! For a mile or more beneath Cherokee Heights the cliff is pierced by caves. Many of them are protected by doors. Some are integrated with houses. Some are living-places themselves with a housefront built on. Some are used as stables or storage vaults, some as garages.

And how popular they will all be in case of atomic attack!

One great cave dug five hundred feet back into the cliff is walled across the front to resemble a castle complete with turrets and battlements. This was used as an underground night-club and was sumptuously fitted with chandeliers, mirrors and objects of art from Gates Mansion, home of an eccentric millionaire.

Evidently it was too cold and clammy for the customers and it is now no longer a night-club but is used as a vault for the storing and ageing of fine cheeses, appropriately trade-named Cavqurd. With the manager's daughter, who seldom sees the light, we walked over damp floors between long rows of ageing cheeses which are said to mature much better below than above ground. With the cheese caves of France in mind, the experiments were here begun by the division of dairy husbandry of the University of Minnesota. Now the business is on a commercial basis and cave-ripened cheeses are shipped all over the United States.

Mushrooms also like the dark. Adjoining caves were used for growing mushrooms, but now they are produced in a nearby cement building, dark as Tophet within, where the spores are embedded in sterilized horse-manure and each day the mature ones are picked by men and women who look like miners because of the electric torches fixed to their foreheads. After being picked, the mushrooms are stored in the caves until needed for shipment. The firm sells $100,000 worth of the great white beauties a year.

You may walk for hours underground. The soft sandstone upon which the city is built is easily cut away and there are said to be twenty miles of tunnels under St Paul.

*　　*　　*

Russian rivalry in scientific achievements has made America painfully conscious of the need for research. Many industries in the Twin Cities are tireless in research.

'Research is the key to tomorrow' is the slogan of the Minnesota Mining and Manufacturing Company, more familiarly known as the 3M.

The research laboratories of the firm occupy large buildings, soon to be further expanded to spread over 150 acres. Twelve hundred scientists here labour to find better ways of doing things. They only putter and experiment, and make nothing. But the ideas they turn up take form in huge factories located some miles away in St Paul and in 18 other cities.

Known as the inventors and makers of Scotch Tape, they make more than fifteen hundred different adhesives, are the world's largest sandpaper manufacturers, turn out abrasives of all kinds, rock granule roofing material, the Scotchlite Reflective sheeting that makes road signs gleam in reflected light, Scotch Electrical Tape for insulation, Scotch Magnetic Recording Tape which is displacing film as a medium for transmitting picture and sound, aluminized fabrics that reflect ninety per cent of the heat incurred by fire-fighters and men who work in high-heat industries, a copying machine that produces a copy of a document in two seconds flat, an offset plate that can be processed for printing in five minutes instead of the conventional half-hour, and dozens of other fascinating and ingenious products.

We saw a demonstration of one of their most recent miracles, a preparation to make fabrics stain-repellent. It insulates every fibre so that oil or grease or other staining material will not soak in. Clothing, rugs, upholstery may be treated with it so that they will be proof against the evil designs of spilled ink, salad dressing, oil or contaminator of any sort. Even dust cannot penetrate the fabric but lies loosely on top where a brush or vacuum cleaner can easily remove it.

We talked with 'the Thomas Edison of Minnesota Mining', Richard G. Drew, who invented Scotch Tape. It was this invention that sparked a great proportion of 3M's other inventions and developments.

'The firm was close to bankruptcy in 1921,' said Drew. 'We were all pretty well discouraged. It was some profanity that started us on the road to success.

'One day my attention was attracted by some very picturesque swearing of the manager of an auto painting concern when the gummed strip that had been put on a car preparatory to spray painting was pulled off and took with it the lacquer right down to the metal.'

The trouble was that the adhesive on the tape had dried rock hard, thus firmly cementing the tape to the paint.

Drew remarked to the manager, 'You should have a non-drying tape.'

'Should I?' was the paint man's scornful reply. 'Then why don't you invent one?'

It was a challenge and young Drew took it up. He experimented for several years – tried everything from tar to chewing gum – and finally became aware of the possibilities of crude rubber and succeeded in making a tape that would not dry rock hard.

On his desk top he demonstrated how the tape can be peeled off without injuring the finish.

'Why was it called Scotch Tape?' Mary wanted to know.

Drew smiled. 'There's a story there too. A big car manufacturer wanted to save money in the use of tape on his cars.
So we worked out a plan to use a tape gummed only along one
edge. He got out his order blank and wrote an order for five
thousand rolls. Then he asked me what name he should put
down for the tape. On the spur of the moment I suggested,
only jokingly, that because of the thrifty Scotch trick of putting
adhesive only on the edge it might be called Scotch Tape.
The manufacturer laughed and wrote the name into the
order. I went back to my employers with certain qualms, but
they liked the name and Scotch Tape it has been ever since.'

Devotion to research is characteristic of many industries
of the Twin Cities and is drilled into budding scientists in such
institutions as the University of Minnesota and the Dunwoody
Institute.

The roadside Burma-Shave jingles that revive the sense of
humour of the weary motorist originate in Minneapolis. The
calendars whose glorious full-colour pictures improve upon
nature come from Brown and Bigelow in St Paul. The push-
button was once considered the last word in ease and comfort;
now pushing a push-button is hard labour compared with the
effortless automatic operation of thermostats made in seven
thousand varieties by the Minneapolis-Honeywell Regulator
Company to control furnaces, turn on and off the music in
juke boxes, revolve eggs in incubators, keep skunks out of
chicken houses.

The ink that prints these words probably depends upon
linseed oil derived from flax produced in Minnesota. That
state grows 36 per cent of the nation's flax.

Farmers enjoy city life in the country. Farms have electricity
or bottled gas, running water, mechanical gadgets of every sort.
Cows are milked by electricity. Calves are sired by a syringe.
There is no need to depend upon the whims of a bull. One
veterinarian artificially inseminates two thousand cows a year.

8

Steamboat Memories

WE HAVE NOW come to the river of big boats. The Mississippi from the Twins to the Gulf was once famous for its floating palaces, with great sidewheels or sternwheels, with tall chimneys crowned with iron plumes, with murals and chandeliers and sumptuous cabins and good food and a deep whistle and gay music on the calliope.

There are a few of the old steamboats left. We boarded one, the *Avalon*, at a St Paul dock for an excursion downriver. Away aloft a steam calliope was playing *Cruising Down the River*.

We spotted the captain, introduced ourselves, and asked permission to visit the top deck where normally no passengers are allowed. We wished to photograph the calliope and its player.

'Certainly – and you'd better hurry. He won't play after we start.'

The high-pressure music was to attract customers and must surely be effective for it could be heard anywhere within a half-mile radius.

We climbed to the top deck. The musician proved to be 22-year-old Clark Hawley, first mate and musician.

'This calliope and one on the *Delta Queen* are the last still in use on the Mississippi,' he said. 'The *Admiral* has one but has nobody to play it – so they use recordings, some of them mine.'

'How old is this instrument?'

'About half a century. It was made a little before 1900.'

The calliope consisted of a row of steam whistles, each connected with a valve, every valve governed by a key on a keyboard like that of an organ. As each key was pressed the corresponding whistle let off a shrill note and a jet of steam.

Mary asked, 'Is it like playing the piano?'

'Well, it's harder. You see, there are fifty-five pounds pressure on each valve.'

It takes strong fingers and a strong back to play the calliope, and ears that will stand more violent sound waves than a hundred symphony orchestra instruments could produce.

As we pulled away from the dock the music stopped. The lusty advertising had done its work and could do no more. The giant stern wheel began churning up the water like the wheel of an old-fashioned grist mill and in the spray that was tossed to the upper decks we could see a rainbow.

The mate took us to the pilot-house. The pilot, Captain Roy Wethern, slim, agile, looked ten or fifteen years younger than his actual age of seventy-five. He got his licence when he was twenty-one.

The *Avalon* is governed by an eight-foot steering wheel, 'the only wheel still in action on the Mississippi with one possible exception,' said Wethern. Modern river-boats are steered by small levers.

The old-fashioned engine telegraph is still in use on the *Avalon*. On modern towboats the pilot does not signal orders to the engineer – he has all the engine controls under his own hands.

The pilot was particularly proud of the fine deep-throated whistle. He operated it by standing on a pedal – only his full weight would make it blow. On the new-fangled boats the pilot touches a button.

We went down to the main deck to talk with the captain. He did not go near the pilot-house. It was the pilot's job to run the boat. The captain's job was administrative. He must look after the crew, the passengers, the dance band, the supplies of food for the snack bars, the finances, the general management of this floating pleasure house.

'It keeps me busy,' he said. 'The capacity of this boat is thirteen hundred passengers. We have a crew of forty-eight. We do no overnight business, just excursions – one in the afternoon, one in the evening, and a third excursion on Saturday or rather Sunday morning sailing at 12.30 a.m., back at 2.30. This is called the Midnight Frolic and, believe me, it's just that when a few hundred teenagers get a little too much beer. We sell no other liquor, just beer, and it isn't sold to the young folks – but they contrive to get someone older to buy it for them. We have to have restaurant facilities for more than a thousand people who will want to eat. On the deck above this we have a 200-foot floor for free dancing and a coloured orchestra that can turn out everything from the *Missouri Waltz* to rock-'n-roll.'

The boat lies all winter at its home port, Cincinnati. It sails from the first of April until the end of September, from town to town, spending one day each at the smaller towns, several days at some, ten days at St Paul. In every sense it is a going concern.

'To pay our way we need five hundred passengers a day. With our two trips a day and three on Saturday we average out at around fifteen hundred passengers a day. So as long as the old boat holds together we can make money and give pleasure to a lot of folks.'

It is good to see some survival of the steamboat era that is still prospering and is likely to stay.

Early inhabitants of the Mississippi navigated the river in baskets, like the coracles still used on some rivers in Wales. The basket was round, some four or five feet in diameter, made of a wicker frame covered with a buffalo's hide. The boat usually carried only one person, two at the most.

When white fur-traders invaded the valley they adopted the Indian craft but enlarged it. They called it a 'bullboat' because of the use of skins of buffalo bulls. These made a sort of rawhide armour plate that would stand a great deal of chafing against the rocks of the river bottom without abrasion. The hides were sewn together into one great sheet which was thoroughly soaked, then placed over the framework where it dried and shrank until it was as tight as a drumhead.

The seams were pitched with a mixture of buffalo tallow and ashes. The boats so built were commonly about 30 feet long. A cargo of six thousand pounds could be carried. The hide became soaked during the day and some water might leak in, therefore at evening when camp was made the boat was unloaded, brought up on the bank and turned bottom up to dry. Here it served as a night shelter for the crew.

Indians of Lake Superior used canoes of cedar wood and birch bark. The early white explorers and traders used them too, but again were not satisfied until they had increased their size and carrying capacity. At the height of the fur trade canoes were built to carry five tons or more.

The pirogue was a canoe, but all in one piece, carved from a huge cypress log. Famous pirogue makers could make a pirogue in two days. Said one such expert,

'It's easy to make a pirogue from a fine log like this. You just chop away the wood you don't need and there's the pirogue. It was inside that log all the time.'

The timber age brought in the lumber raft. It was a way of getting the logs to market. Several thousand logs were bolted together to form a floating island some two or three acres in extent and shanties were thrown up on it to serve as bunkhouses and cookhouse for the crew who must row the raft to its destination.

Cooking was not easy on a raft. Supplies were sometimes

hard to get and the meals were not as bountiful as in a lumber camp.

On a raft commanded by the fabulous Whisky Jack the crew complained about the meals. There was no variety. It was the same old stuff every day. Captain Whisky Jack asked the cook, Big John, why he didn't use a cookery book.

'I got one,' said Big John, 'but I can't do anything with it.'

'Is it too fancy for you?'

'Sure is,' replied Big John. 'Every recipe begins the same way, "Take a clean dish". That stumps me.'

The Wisconsin Folklore Society has resurrected this amusing item on Whisky Jack:

'Whisky Jack was no scholar. He didn't care to read, and he could not write. When he signed the payroll or any other document at the sawmill or lumberyard offices, he signed with a big X instead of his name. He.did this for a long time. But one day he signed with an XX instead of just an X. The book-keeper wondered at this and asked him why he signed with two X's instead of just one. And Whisky Jack explained to him that he and a milliner lady in one of the river towns had just got "spliced", and he thought that now, being a married man, he ought to change his name.'

On some rafts the men took turns doing the cooking. One man cooked until somebody complained. Then the man who complained had to take his place.

A certain temporary cook, Jem Wilson, determined to do the job so badly that the men would get sick of his cooking and let him go back to the oars. He made a batch of biscuits and dumped in enough salt for a barrel of pork. When the men bit into the biscuits one exclaimed,

'Great guns, these here damn biscuits is saltier than hell!'

Suddenly realizing that a complaint would make him the next cook, he hastily added,

'They're the best I ever ate.'

Day and night, the raft went on. If the river was straight

and wide the night watch had little to do and the steersman found it hard to stay awake. One man always held a wrench in his hand. If he fell asleep, the wrench would drop with a clatter on the logs and wake him. Another ingenious steersman hung over his own head a tin can into which water dripped from a valve. When the can filled and overflowed on his head, he woke.

Perhaps because of the monotonous life they led while on board, raftsmen were sons of perdition when they got on shore.

'Raftsmen would just as soon stab you as look at you,' said the hotelkeeper at Le Claire. 'Their real business isn't rafting. Their true calling is battle, murder and sudden death.'

Going down the Mississippi even with the help of the current is not easy, for the prevailing wind is dead against you. Weary oarsmen hailed with delight the invention in 1796 of a boat that replaced manpower with horsepower. It was a side-wheeler whose paddles were turned by eight horses on a treadmill below deck. It worked beautifully, going downstream. It covered the distance from the Ohio to New Orleans with 'prodigious swiftness'. But on the return journey against the current, and with the prevailing wind that did not always prevail, the horses broke down at Natchez. Both boat and horses were abandoned and the crew went home on foot.

One of the oddest of craft on the Mississippi was the wolf-powered ferry remembered by the veteran riverman, Captain Frank J. Fugina:

'A man named Charlie Keith captured two wolf cubs and trained them to swim the river. He made a harness for them and hitched them to a rowboat. These wolves, when full grown, pulled that boat across the fifteen hundred feet of river, carrying passengers who made the trip for the novelty of it. There are fish stories and snake stories, but this is a wolf story and a true one. As a boy I was one of the passengers.'

The problem of how to get back upstream from New

Orleans was presently solved, in a makeshift way at least, by the flatboat. The flatboat went down but didn't try to come back. It was a square-cornered, flat-bottomed craft, roofed over, about a hundred feet long, and looking remarkably like Noah's Ark, especially when it was used to transport cattle, hogs, horses, sheep and fowl as well as inanimate cargo. It was so cheaply put together that it was expendable and at New Orleans it was broken up and sold for lumber, the crew returning by land. During the first third of the nineteenth century as many as three thousand flatboats a year made the one-way trip to New Orleans.

Abe Lincoln, growing up in the river country of the Sangamon, Ohio, and Mississippi, did his turn at flatboating. While drifting downstream he trolled for catfish and sold his catch to planters. On one plantation the overseer refused to allow Abe to see the owner unless he first agreed to divide the take.

'How much do you want?' asked Abe.

'I want half of whatever you get.'

Abe agreed. He was taken into the presence of the owner and delivered his fish.

'How much do you want for them?' asked the planter.

'I want a hundred lashes, well laid on.'

The mystified planter, knowing Abe's curious sense of humour, proceeded to oblige, but instructed the man wielding the lash to go easy. Abe bared his back and took fifty lashes. Then he cried:

'Wait! I've got a partner in this business. Your overseer wouldn't let me in unless I promised to give him half of whatever I get. I reckon the rest belong to him.'

The grafter got his fifty.

Craft of the flatboat type were often used as shopboats. One was a floating drygoods store, one a complete blacksmith's shop, one a tinware factory, and one a floating foundry for the manufacture of axes, scythes and shovels.

There were floating groceries, saloons, and barber shops. There was a circus boat large enough for horsemen, acrobats and trapeze artists. There were floating churches peddling bizarre doctrines and soliciting contributions from the faithful. There were floating theatres that not infrequently sold tickets and then sailed away before show time. It was not too difficult to circumvent the law. Since the Mississippi itself was the boundary line between states, all that was necessary was to sail to the other bank to escape jurisdiction.

Then there were the love boats. They did so much business that they were usually made of two flatboats joined together. On this platform were erected a dancehall, a saloon and a brothel. These floating dives distributed venereal diseases with a lavish hand up and down the great valley. Their chief customers were the raftsmen and lumbermen whose woman-less lives made them eager victims to the primal urges of lust and liquor.

The flatboat's successor was the keelboat which, as its name implied, had a keel to improve its navigability. It was long, slim and trim, and could make a two-way trip, though only with great labour. The keelboat was some seventy feet long and cost two or three thousand dollars. It was too good to throw away. After discharging its cargo at New Orleans it turned about and struggled back upstream. The oars were supplemented by sails which sometimes consisted only of blankets or a screen made of boards. Poles were used in shallow stretches. When the boat hugged the shore the crew laid hold of bushes and branches and pulled the boat along. This process was called 'bushwhacking'. If there was a path along the shore, the crew 'cordelled' the boat by walking up the path pulling the boat after them at the end of a rope.

The tale is told of an Irishman who wanted to get from Ste Genevieve to St Louis. He asked the captain of an upbound boat if he might work his passage. The captain consented and the Irishman took his carpet-bag aboard and settled down

The new-born Mississippi as it issues from Lake Itasca is ankle-deep and so narrow that a bobcat may clear it in one jump. Later in its course it is a mile wide and can swell to a width of eighty miles during flood. The entire Mississippi water-web drains forty per cent of the United States and 13,000 square miles of Canada.

Lumbertown is an authentic replica of a Minnesota lumber town of the 1870s. Its inhabitants are not a century old, but their costumes are, and the General Store stocks tallow candles, fur caps, chamber pots, calomel tea, whiffletrees and bootjacks.

Five cents extra if you want your tooth-pulling alleviated by whisky in Lumbertown's tonsorial and dental parlor.

In the Last Turn Saloon, transferred bodily to Lumbertown, the rotgut is still potent, the palm-reading machines are as genuine a fake as ever and on the tree outside two Indians were hanged in a hurry only to be found innocent an hour later.

Lumbering is not yet dead on the Mississippi. Logs wait to be ground into pulp in a Grand Rapids paper mill. For every tree cut down, a seedling is planted.

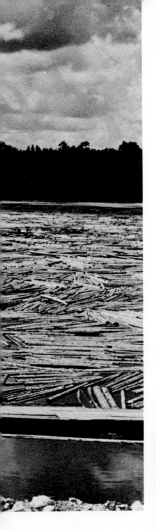

The college student who works at Lumbertown during summer vacation may not be much like Paul Bunyan, mythical lumberjack so big that it took five storks to deliver him, and so strong that he could cut down a forest with one blow of his ax, but he can build a log cabin true to the original.

The showboat, *Mississippi Melodie,* draws up to a woodland stage on the Minnesota shore. The seventy actors disembark and present an old-fashioned variety show to the applause of several hundred spectators.

Men of the National Guard at Camp Ripley span the Mississippi with a pontoon bridge, a difficult task because of strong currents.

In the quarries of St. Cloud the largest such operations in the world produce granite for skyscrapers and tombstones.

The oldtime tombstone sculptor would turn over in his grave if he knew that the once laborious job of lettering and design on marble is now accomplished in a fraction of the time by sand blasting.

Mushrooms like the dark. Lush white beauties are grown in the caves of St. Paul. Other caves are used as homes, restaurants, stables or garages. The soft sandstone underlying the city is easily cut away and there are twenty miles of tunnels beneath St. Paul.

A cavern five thousand feet deep served for years as an underground nightclub. Losing popularity because of its damp chill, it was converted into a vault for the curing and aging of fine cheeses. The manager's daughter dresses warmly, seldom sees the light of day.

The *Avalon* survives the steamboat age. The Mississippi was once famous for floating palaces, with great sidewheels or sternwheels, tall chimneys crowned with iron plumes, murals and chandeliers and sumptuous cabins and good food, a deep-throated whistle and ear-splitting music on the steam calliope. The *Avalon* is still a going concern, carrying thirteen hundred passengers on daily excursions.

A "dredge" is a common thing, but a Mississippi dredge is quite uncommon. This one would cost three million dollars to replace. The "cutter head" (*foreground*) descends to the river bottom and cuts the hard deposits which are then sucked up by an exaggerated vacuum cleaner and blown through a tube sometimes an eighth of a mile long to shore.

for a comfortable journey. But he was promptly ordered
ashore and put at the end of a rope with the rest of the crew.
After three miles of trudging and sweating under the hot sun
he complained,

'So you call this a boat trip. Faith, I'd about as soon walk.'

*   *   *

But something was happening that would soon make oars,
poles, sails, bushwhacking and the cordelle unnecessary.

The age of steam did not come suddenly. Nor did it begin
with James Watt and his tea-kettle. The ingenious Greeks
in the second century B.C. devised a steam engine and used
it to open and close the heavy doors of temples. Leonardo da
Vinci was one of many who experimented with steam. In the
sixteenth century a Spanish captain devised a steamboat
and sailed it in the harbour of Barcelona. In the seventeenth
an Italian engineer made a steam windmill. A mining engineer
used steam to drain the mines of Cornwall.

It was a century later before Watt, studying the behaviour
of his tea-kettle, improved the steam engine by adding a
separate condenser.

A mild and timid man who went from door to door cleaning
and mending clocks was the next genius in the history of steam.
It seemed to him that Watt's contraption could be used to
propel a boat. In a blacksmith's shop John Fitch put together
a clumsy thing made of scraps of metal and wood and tried
it out on the Delaware. It actually worked, but not very well.

He tried to get financial help, from Congress, from capital-
ists, from anybody, but failed. Perhaps France would be
interested. He scraped together enough money to pay his
passage to France, got nothing but polite smiles when he
talked about driving a boat by steam, and had to work his
passage home. He left his design with the United States
Consul in France.

That gentleman was later visited by a young American artist, Robert Fulton. The conversation got around to fantastic inventions and the consul, to amuse his guest, brought out the steamboat drawings. Fulton got permission to keep them for several months.

Meanwhile John Fitch, penniless but persistent, built a steamboat out of an old yawl. The boiler was a ten-gallon iron pot and the cylinders were wooden barrels. He tried out the boat on Collect Pond in New York City but, although it made several circuits of the pond under its own power, it was not taken seriously by anyone except John Fitch.

He wandered to Kentucky, built a small model of a steamboat three feet long and ran it on a stream at Bardstown. Again he reaped nothing but amusement. He hoarded the opium pills his doctor had been giving him to make him sleep and when he had a dozen he swallowed them with a glass of whisky. That was the end of John Fitch and his dreams of steam.

But Fulton had been set to dreaming and the result was a successful demonstration of the *Clermont* on the Hudson River. Navigation of other eastern rivers soon followed. Fulton with two partners decided to try the Mississippi. In Pittsburgh they built and launched the *New Orleans,* a handsome blue sidewheeler. She sailed down to her namesake city without difficulty, but her engines were too feeble to bring her up against the current and her deep keel, patterned after the keel of ocean vessels, was not adapted to shallow water.

Her captain, Henry Shreve, saw what was the matter. A Mississippi steamer must sail on the water, not in it. A few years later he built his own steamboat, flatbottomed, drawing so little water that amazed rivermen said it would 'float on dew'. His *Washington* had a high-pressure engine and was the first steam-driven vessel on the Mississippi to go upstream as well as down.

That did it. The last doubter was convinced. Shippers

clamoured for cargo space on the *Washington*. The keelboat
followed the flatboat into oblivion. Boat-builders by the
dozen began to turn out steamers. From that year, 1816, to
the end of the century, the steamboat was queen of the
Mississippi.

Shreve had not only initiated a style of travel that was
practical, it was also good fun. Before this a river journey had
been an uncomfortable experience. But the *Washington* was
luxury afloat, the public rooms were elaborate with carved
woodwork and mirrors, soft carpets and fine furniture, the
meals were as good as could be had in the best hotels and
were served with a fine flourish.

Other builders took their cue from Shreve and went on to
outdo him. Boats rapidly grew longer and lovelier. Their
saloons glittered with cut-glass chandeliers and glowed with
oil paintings. Bronze and marble statues lent an air of culture.
The dining-room gleamed with solid silver and as many as
two dozen stewards were in attendance. A typical menu was
two feet long and offered thirteen desserts.

The *Eclipse* eclipsed its predecessors by providing forty-
eight bridal chambers, a grand piano and provision for the
lordly planter who wished to take along a full retinue of
servants.

'The steamboats were finer than anything on shore,' wrote
Mark Twain in *Life on the Mississippi*. 'When a citizen stepped
on board a big fine steamboat he entered a new and marvel-
ous world.'

There was always an elaborate and well-stocked bar, and
not only gambling tables but professional gamblers who could
be trusted to make one's trip memorable.

The boat was as handsome without as within. Her lines
were sweet. She sat lightly on the water like a swan. Her twin
smokestacks towered high and their tops were scalloped to
look like feathers or ferns. On her sides appeared her name in
gold leaf and sometimes above the name a landscape or

mythical figure. She was decked with colourful flags, that of the line on the jackstaff, burgees bearing the names of the cities visited, the union jack on the flagstaff at the rear of the texas deck, and on the rear flagstaff the Stars and Stripes. She never made port without music produced by calliope or orchestra and most of the town was at the dock to meet her.

When the first note of her whistle or bell was heard even the worshippers in churches slipped out and headed for the landing. A church wedding had proceeded up to the point of 'Will you have this woman—?' when a steamboat whistle was heard. The church emptied like magic and the minister, seeing that even the bridal couple were anxious to be off, said with as much dignity as he could muster,

'The remainder of the service will be completed at the steamboat landing.'

Travel on a Mississippi steamboat was not only sumptuous, it could be highly exciting. One never knew when the boiler would blow up. Between 1810 and 1850 there were four thousand steamboat casualties, most of them due to boiler explosions. Mark Twain's brother, Henry Clemens, was one of a hundred who lost their lives when four of the *Pennsylvania*'s eight boilers exploded. Boats foundered on snags or sandbars. Or someone dropped a cigarette and the wooden structure loaded with bales of inflammable cotton went up like a torch. The average life of a steamboat was reckoned at four to five years and it could be fairly sure of coming to a violent end.

The Marquis de Lafayette, remembered for his aid in the American Revolution, made a return visit to America in 1824. One night as he was on his way upriver aboard the steamboat *Mechanic* the boat suddenly ran into a snag and stopped so abruptly that passengers were thrown from their berths. The hull was torn open by the impact and the boat immediately began to sink.

The first thought of the officers was to get their famous guest ashore, but Lafayette refused to leave until the women and children had been taken off. Then, as he was about to step into a small boat, he remembered that he had left behind a snuff box decorated with a portrait of George Washington. So deep had been his affection for his old associate that he had named his own son Georges Washington Lafayette. Now, as the packet listed perilously, burying the lower deck under water, he would not leave until he had recovered this precious memento.

Then he was rowed ashore and provided with a soggy mattress on which he spent the rest of the night under a steady rain. In the morning some damp biscuits and smoked venison were retrieved from the wreck and had to serve as breakfast for the sodden survivors. The hardy old general was the liveliest of the lot and refused to allow the mortified captain to blame himself for the accident. It was late in the morning before the steamboat *Paragon* noticed the wreck, picked up the shivering castaways, got them into dry clothes and landed them at Louisville.

To enquiring newsmen the marquis played down the incident and laughed, 'Just another good story to tell my grandchildren.'

* * *

Quite as calm and collected as Lafayette was the life insurance salesman on the night of the sinking of the *Emilie La Barge*. As the waters rose from deck to deck he hurried about among the jittery passengers selling life insurance. He could hardly make himself heard above the hissing steam due to the flooding of water into the firebox.

'Quit that nonsense!' the captain told him. 'Don't you know that boiler is apt to explode any minute?'

'Perhaps – perhaps not. My company will take a chance.'

It was a chance well taken, for the boiler did not blow up and the boat struck bottom before the top deck was engulfed. There had not been time to get out the yawls. All the twenty-five passengers and thirty crew members together with several dozen cattle and hogs were packed like sardines on the upper deck.

Said Captain Keith, 'Now, folks, we are a good many miles from a city of any size, and we can't arrange transportation for you tonight. We could land you and let you spend the night on shore. But it is my opinion that you would be just as safe up here on the roof of the boat. I suggest you sleep here, and early tomorrow morning we will take you by waggon to the city.'

After some discussion, in which the cattle and hogs joined lustily, a spokesman for the passengers reported,

'We think you are right, Captain. After all, it will be a novelty to sleep on a sunken boat.'

Blankets were provided, but there was no room to lie down and little inclination to sleep. The boat's musicians struck up a tune and the glory of a full moon made the situation almost romantic. There was singing and as much dancing as space would allow and while the water lapped within a few inches of their feet the shipwrecked merrymakers staged the gayest and strangest party of their lives. The next day waggons transported them to the nearest railroad station.

*   *   *

It was not so much of a party when the boiler exploded. This was such a common experience that Charles Dickens, when he visited the river, made sure that his stateroom was in the stern because steamboats generally blew up forward. John Hay memorialized steamboat explosions when he sang of the courage of Jim Bludso who would not leave his boat when the boilers burst but would

> '. . . hold her nozzle agin the bank
> Till the last galoot's ashore.'

There was always an argument between railroad men and rivermen as to the relative safety of their professions. A negro railroad porter clinched the argument to his own satisfaction with this comment,

'If you is blowed up on the railroad, there you is; but, good lord, if you is blowed up on a steamboat, where is you?'

A humorous tale, perhaps not too authentic, is told by W. H. Milburn in a volume published in 1892. It seems that Jim Smith sat in his cabin cleaning his rifle and his wife knitted when suddenly there was a terrible explosion on the river and the next instant a man came through the roof and dropped at their feet. Jim went on cleaning his gun and Mattie kept knitting. The stranger sat up, squinted at the hole in the roof and said,

'Well, my man, what's the damage?'

Jim put down his rifle, took a look at the hole, and said, 'Ten dollars'.

'You be hanged,' said the traveller. 'Last week I was blown up in another steamboat, opposite St Louis, and fell through three floors of a new house and they only charged me five dollars. No, no, my man, I know what the usual figure is in such cases. Here's two dollars – if that won't do, sue me.'

Boat owners lost boats so frequently that they ran out of names. The easiest thing to do in such cases was to keep the name and add a number. The *Zebulon M. Pike* was built in 1817 and blew up before the year was out. It was replaced by the *Pike II*, and that by the *Pike III* and in 1840 the *Pike VIII* was sailing the river – all its predecessors had been blown to bits or burnt. There were seven *Ben Franklin*s. In forty years there were eight *Postboy*s. When Pilot George Merrick came back to the river after fourteen years in the East he found not a single vessel that he had known.

Sometimes boats were destroyed wholesale. Twenty-three steamers, three barges, and forty small craft went up in flames along the waterfront of St Louis on the night of 17 May

1849. A steward had been airing a mattress. A spark from a
passing steamer set fire to the mattress and a strong wind
carried the flames through the fleet.

The Mississippi is a windy river. Cyclones love it. A tornado
struck the *Alexander Mitchell* one midnight interrupting a
Virginia Reel. It happened to be a Sunday night and the
captain, famous for his piety, had objected strongly but in
vain to such frivolity on the part of his guests. The wind
ripped away both smokestacks and tore the roof from the
pilot-house. The mate who had been standing near the ship's
bell was picked up bodily and dropped on shore several hundred feet away. The port lifeboat was blown a mile and a half
across the prairie and came down in a farmer's barnyard.
The steamer shook as with the ague and the panic-stricken
revellers appealed to the captain but he gave them no
comfort.

'That,' he said to them sternly, 'is what comes of dancing.'

Incidentally a considerable number of Mississippi masters
were praying men. Commodore William F. Davidson of the
White Collar Line assembled his crew on deck every Sunday
morning and held a prayer meeting. One of his prayers
concluded with the words,

'And, O Lord, bless the poor. Give to every poor family a
barrel of pork – a barrel of flour – a barrel of sugar – a barrel
of salt – a barrel of pepper.' Then, hesitating for a moment,
he added, 'Oh hell no – that's too much pepper!'

*   *   *

For a generation a tourist attraction was a steamboat
perched on a hilltop twenty miles from the river. It was in
1882 that the *Rosa May* was carried by flood water through a
gap in the levee below Vicksburg and swept through willows
and sycamores and briar patches to stick finally on Bullhorn
Ridge twenty miles inland. When the waters retreated there

it was, very much like Noah's Ark after the flood, perched on its own little Ararat. The owner considered salvage not worth the cost. The boat was a boon to local residents who knew where to go whenever they needed a plank, a door, a lock or a lamp, and there are still homes in the vicinity that owe a part of their furnishings to the *Rosa May*.

*   *   *

The most serious single catastrophe in all the chequered history of the Mississippi was the explosion of the *Sultana* in April, 1865. In loss of life, this disaster ranked among the world's worst half-dozen of all time.

It was only eleven days after the end of the Civil War. Prisoners had been set free by both North and South and were returning to their homes.

The rickety old *Sultana*, once the pride of the river but sadly run down for lack of attention during the struggle, lay alongside the Vicksburg landing. One of her old boilers had a chronic leak.

But because she would carry them home she looked good to the 2,134 Union soldiers who climbed aboard her on that bright April morning. Her captain looked on apathetically. He knew he was taking aboard a thousand too many passengers, but he was under orders. There were no private quarters for such a number. Men sat huddled close together on the decks, happy after the discomforts of prison to breathe the fresh air and feel the sun.

The *Sultana* moved sluggishly upriver. Badly overloaded, she had all she could do to get enough power from her weakened boilers. The leak grew steadily worse and at dusk the boat stopped at Memphis for repairs. A patch was applied and the boat went on, despite the engineer's comment:

'T'won't do any good. What you need is a new boiler.'

Crewmen of the gunboat *Grosbeak*, moored in Memphis

harbour exchanged shouts of greeting and farewell with the happy passengers of the *Sultana* as she resumed her journey north. They watched her lights dwindle to pinpoints in the darkness. Then they saw a sudden burst of flame illuminate the entire river and an instant later heard a deafening thunder to equal any artillery bombardment they had known during the war. The explosion was followed by a steady glare, the brilliant holocaust of the burning steamboat.

The gunboat immediately got under way but could not come close to the floating bonfire because of the terrific heat. Everywhere floated the bodies of men thrown in all directions by the explosion. Some survivors clung to boards, barrels, fragments of the lifeboats, anything that would float. These were rescued, but scores of drifting army caps told the story of men who were already dead when they struck the water or were so stunned by the explosion that they immediately drowned.

The death toll was 1,550. It would be 47 years before this death record of Americans by shipwreck would be equalled, or nearly equalled, by the *Titanic* with the loss of 1,513. The name of that ship is engraved in public memory, as is also that of the *Lusitania* with a death toll of 1,198.

But who remembers the *Sultana*? The incident was forgotten almost at once, for the front pages of newspapers were taken up with the assassination of Abraham Lincoln and the death of the assassin, John Wilkes Booth. And the public had known such a succession of horrors during a long and terrible war, such endless lists of war dead, that this final loss found sensibilities already numbed by disaster.

The wreck of the *Sultana* still lies where she sank. Nobody knows where that is. Since then the Mississippi has changed its course and the site of the sinking must lie far inland deep under the sedimentary soil of Arkansas, its human ashes rising to life again in farms and forests. In 1955 excavations were made in the hope of finding at least the metal remains of the exploded boilers and engines, but without success.

*   *   *

In spite of disasters, public demand for river travel kept growing and steamboats became fancier and faster. A speed mania took possession of the river. It was the ambition of every boat to 'take the horns'. Who originated the custom is not known, but a pair of gilded deer antlers was awarded by a committee of judges to the fastest boat on the Mississippi. The antlers were proudly mounted on the front of the pilot-house. No boat owned these horns and they could be worn only during the period of her championship. Any boat making a faster trip took the horns. The transfer was made at a grand banquet and ball of river society.

Previously a broom had been used for the same purpose. Nailed to the pilot-house, it gave notice that the boat bearing it had made a 'clean sweep' of the river. This custom was not original with the Mississippi. It had long been known on the high seas. The replacement of the broom with antlers provided a symbol more appropriate to the great river of the western forests where deer could be seen almost daily and were loved for their grace and speed.

The risks were many in every race to capture the antlers. Barrels of resin were tossed into the fireboxes and sent the flames hissing and roaring through the flues. Casks of salt pork were a favourite fuel. Boilers became red-hot and the paint blistered on the chimneys. Firemen were plied with whisky to make them indifferent to danger. Safety valves were tied down, choking off the escaping steam, and increasing the pressure in the boilers close to the bursting point. Too often that point was passed and an explosion ended the race.

The most famous of all the contests was the one between the *Natchez* and the *Robert E. Lee* in June of 1870.

It was a contest between two men as well as two boats. The captains were sworn enemies. They accused each other of cargo-stealing. They had beaten each other into a state of semi-consciousness in a New Orleans saloon.

Old Tom Leathers had red hair and a pirate beard and a hot temper, together with a strict sense of honour. Stocky, black-bearded John Cannon was reckless and shrewd. His war record had left something to be desired.

Instead of contributing his former vessel, the *General Quitman*, to the Confederate cause, he had cannily removed it out of the path of war up the Red River. There he bought up cotton from desperate planters at rock-bottom prices and, as soon as the conflict was over, took it down to the Mississippi and sold it at an enormous profit. With this shady fortune he built the beautiful *Robert E. Lee*.

Captain Leathers, on the other hand, had turned his vessel over to the Confederate Army and had seen it burned to water level by the bluecoats. He regarded Cannon as a traitor and had no hesitation in telling him so.

He had further annoyed his competitor by capturing the golden antlers. His *Princess* had broken all records and he claimed that his new boat, *Natchez*, was even faster.

On that historic night the two boats were due to pull out of New Orleans at the same time. There had been no announcement that they would race, but the rumour had spread through the city and the docks were crowded with spectators.

The *Natchez* had taken on a full complement of cargo and passengers, and guaranteed that all stops would be made as usual. The *Lee* took passengers but no freight and gave notice that the boat would go through to St Louis without a stop.

Even more significant was what the *Lee* had done to lighten her load and reduce wind resistance. To let the air slip through her, glass had been removed from the pilot-house and the doors in front of the saloon as well as the windows aft of the ladies' cabin, the splashboards behind the wheels were gone and anything else that would catch the wind. All dispensable weight, derricks, rigging, spare anchors, mooring chains, were thrown ashore.

The boats were scheduled to leave at 5 p.m. Four minutes before that time the *Lee* threw off her lines and started upriver. At five sharp the *Natchez* followed.

Now any child who has read a copybook knows that virtue always triumphs. It was only right and natural that the sharp practices of the wily Cannon should fail and that the *Natchez* should pass the *Lee* and win the race.

The telegraph took the news to towns upstream and for a thousand miles spectators lined the levees and waterfronts.

At first the *Natchez* steadily gained on the *Lee*. This was taken as impressive evidence that, given equal loading, the *Natchez* was the faster vessel. She drew up within four hundred yards of her competitor.

Then there was an anxious report from the engine-room. Water was spilling from a broken valve and lowering the steam pressure. Captain Leathers took his boat to shore, tied up to a willow, and the engineers worked on the valve while the *Lee* disappeared around the bend.

It was half an hour before Old Tom was once more on his way, Then he was so anxious to make time that he took a short cut and slid up on a sand-bar. The red-whiskered captain was a master of epithets and he made full use of them now.

All passengers were ordered aft to throw weight astern and the reversed engines slowly backed the boat into deep water. Then it was necessary to take the long way around. It all consumed valuable time.

The river was low, bringing shoals near the surface, and since these shoals were constantly changing under the force of the currents it was impossible even for the most experienced master to know precisely what he would find at any given point. Luck was a large ingredient in river travel, and luck again played Captain Leathers false when it rammed his boat on another sand-bar and held it fast for twenty minutes.

At dawn, almost out of fuel, the *Natchez* came alongside barges and stopped to load coal. This was the normal procedure and Captain Leathers had sworn he would make his trip in the normal fashion.

But Captain Cannon, bound by no such inhibitions, had made arrangements for refuelling without so much as a slow-down. Near Greenville the fast steamer *Pargaud*, winner of several races, came alongside, lashed fast, and transferred 120 cords of pine knots to the *Lee* while both vessels kept up a full head of steam. At Memphis coal was taken on in the same manner. At Cairo where the *Lee* ordinarily would have docked she forged straight ahead while the *Idlewild* drew up beside her and contributed eighty passengers and their baggage.

Now it was the *Lee*'s turn to have engine trouble. An over-strained and overheated boiler promised to blow up. Cannon would not stop for repairs. The *Lee* pounded ahead, her human freight poised on the edge of Kingdom Come.

A night and a day and a night and no sleep for either master. Then a new anxiety – fog. It was so thick that one could not see a boat's length ahead and radar had not yet been born. The boats were entering the 'Graveyard Stretch', infamous for its shallows, rocks and shoals. The *Lee* blindly ploughed on. The captain of the *Natchez*, conscious of his responsibility to his ninety passengers and crew, tied up to the bank. The race was lost and they knew it. So they slept.

The *Lee* poked on, slowing down, sending a small boat ahead to make soundings. In spite of these precautions the steamer several times ran up on bars that dangerously ground into her hull, but she managed to back away and continue.

Three days, eighteen hours and fourteen minutes after leaving New Orleans the *Lee* trumpeted her arrival to the crowds massed on the St Louis waterfront and the steamboat's deep whistle was answered with shouts, cannon shots, and general uproar from every steamboat whistle and calliope in the harbour.

It was a record and is still a record, unbroken even by modern towboats. The *Lee* got the horns. The *Natchez* trailed in the next day. Her time was four days and ten minutes.

Yet the case is still argued in waterfront bars all the way from New Orleans to St Louis. Yes, say the friends of the *Natchez*, the *Lee* got there first. But if you subtract the time the cautious Captain Leathers stopped for repairs, stopped for fuel, stopped for fog, stopped for passengers and freight, you can prove – so they say – that the *Natchez* was the faster boat.

*   *   *

Why did the exciting and luxurious floating palaces of the Mississippi disappear?

The impatient age arrived, people were in a hurry, roads and railroads offered faster transportation.

Rivermen feared and resented the iron monsters on wheels. The tracks ended at the river's edge. There the train stopped and the one-eyed locomotive stared down disdainfully at passing boats. Passengers were ferried across the river and stepped into another train on the other side. Before their eyes, steamboat men saw their livelihood slipping away from them.

The crowning insult was the proposal to fling bridges across the river so that trains might go through without delay. Bridges would stand on piers, and piers would put serious hazards in the way of river traffic. Vessels were bound to be wrecked. During high water boats with lofty stacks would not be able to get through under the span.

In spite of a hailstorm of protests, the Rock Island Railroad in 1855 spanned the river with a bridge between Rock Island and Davenport. The next year the *Effie Afton* struck a pier of the bridge, caught fire and sank, taking a part of the bridge down with it. There was much loss of life, both human and bovine, for the sidewheeler had carried a full list of passengers and oxen.

The owners of the sunken steamboat sued the Rock Island Railroad. The defence lawyer engaged by the railroad was a certain young Abraham Lincoln of Springfield.

This born and bred riverman prepared his case with skill. In a rowboat he drifted under and around the broken bridge studying angles and currents. In waterfront bars where crewmen's tongues sometimes wagged a little too freely under the influence of liquor, he learned that one of the paddlewheels of the *Effie* had not been working on the day of the accident, thus making the vessel hard to steer. The boat should not have proceeded until the wheel was repaired. With a dead starboard wheel and an offshore current, the crash was inevitable.

So he argued when the case came to trial in Chicago. He seemed to destroy his own case by admitting freely that the bridge was an obstruction. Moreover it was built at the wrong angle with reference to the currents, and when rebuilt this should be taken into consideration.

'Lincoln has lost the case for us,' said one of the associate counsel at the end of the first day of the trial. 'The admissions he made in regard to the currents will convince the court that a bridge at that point will always be a serious and constant detriment to navigation on the river.'

But Lincoln's admissions demonstrated his own fairness and took the wind out of the sails of the prosecuting attorney. Lincoln went on to discuss the right of the railroad to build this, the first railroad bridge over the Mississippi. The pith of his argument was that one man had as good a right to cross a river as another had to sail up or down it. Just as each has the right to cross a street or pass along it.

'Must the products of all the boundless fertile country lying west of the river for all time be compelled to stop on its western bank, be unloaded from the cars and loaded upon a boat and, after the transit across the river, be reloaded into cars on the other side, to continue their journey east?'

He painted in bright colours the future of the great West and urged that nothing should be allowed to stay the progress of development and civilization in that promised land.

The steamboat company lost its case against the railroad. The bridge was rebuilt, but angled properly to the natural flow of the stream. It continued to be a possible obstruction, as were all the bridges that came after it, and rivermen still grumble, but no longer question the need of bridges. Lincoln has been called the author of the American doctrine of bridges.

As railroads and highway development cut in on steamboat profits, river towns unintentionally joined in the destruction of the very traffic that kept them alive. They charged steamboats such heavy dues for the privilege of using their wharves that boats could not afford to stop unless there were enough passengers or bales of cargo to be transferred to cover the cost of wharfage.

The golden age of the steamboat lasted only some eighty years. Even as early as 1874 a former pilot, who had known the river in its exciting heyday, noted its dreary return to primitive emptiness.

'We met two steamboats at New Madrid,' wrote the author of *Life on the Mississippi*. 'Two steamboats in sight at once! An infrequent spectacle now in the lonesome Mississippi. The loneliness of this solemn, stupendous flood is impressive – and depressing. League after league, and still league after league, it pours its chocolate tide along, between its solid forest walls, its almost untenanted shores, with seldom a sail or a moving object of any kind to disturb the surface and break the monotony of the blank, watery solitude.'

* * *

But a few delightful reminders of the steamboat age persist even to the present day.

We have mentioned the *Avalon*. It is not the only paddle-wheeler to survive on the Mississippi, nor is it even the most important one. The *Admiral* sailing out of St Louis is twice as big and carries four times as many passengers. In all we were to see twenty-seven paddlewheelers, four of them resting ashore, all the others still afloat. They included the *Delta Queen*, *Sprague*, *West*, *Arkansas*, *Mississippi*, *Patrick Hurley*, *Memphis Belle*, *Avalon*, *Pearson*, four stern-wheel houseboats, the showboat *Mississippi Melodie II*, the showboat *Goldenrod* the *Bemidji Belle*, *Ste Genevieve*, *Pelican*, *Admiral*, *President*, *Lone Star*, *W. J. Quinlan*, *Pearl*, *Addie May*, *Fruitland Ferry*, *General Newton* and sternwheeler of the Sea Scouts.

However, this was the result of five months' investigation of the entire length of the river. It is probable that the average resident of a Mississippi town whose interests seldom take him to the river does not see a paddlewheeler from one year's end to the next: he is quite justified in supposing this vessel to have vanished completely from the river.

But he does know about the towboat. In that respect he is one ahead of most Americans who are aware only that the glorious days of the steamboat era have passed and therefore visualize the Mississippi as a dead and empty thoroughfare whose job has been taken over by the train, the truck and the aeroplane.

9

Miracle of the Towboat

THE STEAMBOAT ERA is gone, but the Mississippi is not dead. It is more alive than at any time in its history. Its youth and strength have been renewed. It now does in a day what it once did in a year. For the Mississippi's new usefulness we must thank the towboat.

The towboat is misnamed. The word 'towboat' gives no idea of the nature of this remarkable craft. One is apt to confuse it with a tugboat – the busy little beetle that hauls barges across New York Harbor or presses its padded nose against the bow or stern of an ocean liner hugging up to a North River dock.

The towboat is nothing like that. It is one of the miracles of the transportation age. Instead of one deck it may have five or more. Instead of one engine it is likely to have four. Instead of one rudder it has ten. Instead of a few hundred horsepower it will deliver four to eight thousand. Instead of nudging an ocean liner it will push a fleet of barges carrying the load of two great ocean-going freighters. Instead of carrying a crew of two or three men it requires seventeen or twenty. Instead of costing a few thousand dollars, its owners consider it cheap if they can get it built for a million.

The towboat is not really a towboat. It is a pushboat. It tows nothing.

In the long-distant past it did haul its barges behind it

and was properly called a towboat. The name has stuck, although the method of handling a tow has changed.

A string of barges trailing out behind could not be controlled. It whipped about like a crocodile's tail. Cross-currents or cross-winds threw it onto the rocks or into other boats or against bridge piers.

So the barges were put in front instead of behind. Barges perhaps three abreast and numbering a dozen or more were tied together so rigidly by steel cables that they became one unyielding raft and this tow (still called a tow although it was to be pushed) was locked in place before the towboat and so firmly integrated with it by steel cables that the entire fleet became a single unit subject to the slightest touch of the pilot upon the steering levers.

Push towing, thanks to the Mississippi example, is now being initiated in lands as far apart as Laos, Germany and Argentina. Mississippi captains have been called abroad to teach the new method on the Mekong, the Rhine and the Plata.

The barge, like the towboat, is too humbly named. The Mississippi barge is a floating warehouse. One jumbo-size barge costs $90,000 to build. A standard barge weighs about three hundred tons and will carry a thousand in cargo.

Recently built barges dwarf these figures. A hopper barge now in operation has a capacity in excess of twenty-five hundred tons. A single barge will carry the load of three or four of the large packets of steamboat days. And one towboat may push twenty or more such barges!

One grain barge will carry a hundred thousand bushels. One tank barge will take a million gallons of oil. (By comparison, a railroad tank car has a capacity of ten thousand gallons.)

An integrated tow, the entire unit lashed together to make one streamlined vessel, may stretch to twelve hundred feet – longer than the largest ocean liner afloat. The *Queen Elizabeth* stops at 1,031 feet, the *Queen Mary* at 1,019.

Such a tow can carry two hundred thousand barrels (thirty-five thousand tons) of oil, the equivalent of the load of two ocean-going tankers.

This fabulous development in the history of transportation began during the first World War. Half a century before, the railroads had banished the steamboats. The river was rediscovered in 1917. The demands of war overwhelmed the railroads. The government commandeered the few barges and towboats that could be found on the Mississippi, hastily built a fleet of new boats, and formed what became known as the Federal Barge Lines.

Great stores of war materials began to move. Private investors saw the opportunity and formed barge lines of their own. The government, having demonstrated what could be done, sold the Federal Barge Lines to private investors in 1953. The firm retained the same name but was now on its own and had plenty of competition. There were now more than 150 privately-owned barge companies on the Mississippi system. There was plenty of business for all and it continues to grow spectacularly year by year.

* * *

Through the courtesy of the Federal Barge Lines we are put aboard the towboat *Huck Finn*. She was originally steam-powered but has now been converted to diesel.

People who confuse towboats with tugboats should see this vessel. It is only of average size, yet instead of the single deck of a tugboat, there are six levels in the *Huck Finn* – the radar deck on top, the pilothouse level, the texas deck, the boiler deck, the main deck, and the below-water engine-room deck.

But she has to be big and powerful to push the equivalent of a heavily loaded train four miles long, and that's about what her twenty thousand tons of cargo would amount to. That is only a modest load for a modern tow. In the pilot-house I pick up today's paper and happen to see an item concerning a tow of twenty-four barges, 126,000 square feet or almost three acres, now being pushed on the Tennessee River by the towboat *Robin*, 3,200 horsepower. Three acres on the move! I read the item aloud to the pilot. He says,

'Imagine how hard it would be to stop it.' He is peering anxiously ahead because this is Sunday and the small boats are out in force. They skip across the river in front of our tow.

'They have a lot of confidence in their motors,' remarks the pilot. 'If their power failed while they were ahead of us nothing in the world could prevent us from running them down. We could reverse our engines, but with the momentum of twenty thousand tons plus the force of the current we couldn't stop in less than a quarter of a mile.'

Half an hour later the pilot's fears are borne out. A motorboat flashes in front of the tow hauling a water skier who loses his balance and falls in the path of the oncoming barges. The pilot immediately throws the engines into reverse and blows a thundering blast on the whistle. There is nothing more he can do. The raft of barges ploughs on remorselessly towards the struggling skier. To the people in other boats it must look as if we are deliberately running the man down. They blow their horns and shout at us, the men angrily, the women hysterically, unaware that the boat's engines are doing their best, though vainly, to check the speed of the fleet.

The man disentangles himself from his skis and begins to swim. He is a good swimmer but he will never make it. The oncoming barges are too broad for him to get out of their path in time.

But there is a man in one of those speedboats who can do something besides blow his horn and shout. He sends his boat roaring into the path of the approaching tow. He slows just long enough to seize the swimmer and haul him aboard.

If his motor should stall now there would be two deaths instead of one. It does not stall and the boat shoots across the front of the barges and into safe water.

Onlookers cheer the rescuer and curse the towboat pilot. The floating skis disappear beneath the raft. They will not look like skis any more after a quarter of a mile of pummelling under the barges and towboat.

The pilot's face is tight and white. He is the one who should have been cursing through this entire episode but he has not said a word. Now he flips the engines back to full ahead and calls for a cup of coffee.

He smiles over his coffee. 'Nearly went to gaol that time.'

'Who, you? It wasn't your fault.'

'The law doesn't look at it that way. The least that could happen would be a trial and a fine and perhaps discharge. One pilot I know has been waiting trial for three months for running over a motorboat. Just last week he had the bad luck to run over another. I'd hate to be in his shoes when he goes to court. It's tricky, this business. Too many things you can't control. To be a pilot you need 10 per cent skill and 90 per cent luck.'

There is always the river to reckon with and Old Man River has many moods. He unexpectedly throws up a sand-bar: the front barges run up on it, break the huge ratchets and steel lines that bind them together, explode in all directions over the river. A petrol barge wraps itself around a bridge abutment and blows up. A barge breaks loose and slips into a side bayou and you spend all night and the next day searching for it until a helicopter pilot sights it and reports its location. The steering gear goes dead as you are trying to make a bend and you go into the rocks with a crash like the end of the world. A snag pokes a hole in a petrol barge and the river all around is covered with a film of petrol, and that's a bad time to light a cigarette.

Recently eighteen men of a towboat crew were killed in collision with a bridge. Ploughing upstream, the ploughing may become too literal and the forward edge of the raft may dive under, drowning any men who happen to be on duty.

And not a few deck-hands have retired because it was not possible to continue their vocation on one leg, the other having been sliced off by a snapping steel line.

The dinner bell rings. The time is fifteen minutes before noon.

'You can eat at the first table or the second,' says the pilot. 'I'd advise the second. Then you won't have to hurry.'

He explains that the meals come at the change of watches. Each watch is six hours long. During one watch half the crew will be in bed, the other half on duty and the pilot will be at the helm. During the next six hours the other half of the crew will be on the job and the captain will come up to the pilot-house and take over from the pilot.

At the end of every six hours during the daytime there is a meal. But it would not do for all the men to eat at one time, leaving the boat at the mercy of the river. So those who have been off duty sit down to table at fifteen minutes before the hour, finish on the hour, and go on watch. They must dispose of a truly gargantuan meal in fifteen minutes. Those who have been on watch come to the table on the hour, finish when they please, sit around and talk a while, then go to bed.

Thus breakfast is at 5.45 or 6 a.m.; dinner (it is too heavy a meal to be called lunch) at 11.45 or 12; and dinner again at 5.45 or 6.

We retired to our stateroom to freshen up for dinner. The *Huck Finn* is not one of the newer boats and the cabin was equipped with two bunks, not beds. But it did have the luxury of a private bath and everything was clean and comfortable.

On the stroke of twelve we sat down with the men who had just come off watch to a table groaning with great bowls of steaming food. The barge lines seem to have taken a leaf from the book of the oldtime lumber camps where it was thought good policy to feed men well so they could work well.

There are several kinds of meat, half a dozen vegetables, five different drinks of which milk seems to be the most popular, a colossal dessert of pie and ice cream and cake. Down the middle of the table is a phalanx of some twenty different kinds of jam as well as bread, rolls, muffins, biscuits and enough pickles, olives, ketchups, sauces and spices to furnish a delicatessen.

We have a woman cook, Stella by name, all smiles – and a mess girl, Jody, very pleasant and thoughtful – and good-looking enough to distract some of the woman-hungry men. One of them rising from the table grabs her around the waist from behind and carries her, squealing and protesting but obviously liking it, out to the deck with the pretence of being about to throw her overboard.

Stella is new, has never been aboard a towboat before, and has never cooked for a lot of men. She does remarkably well. The food is good.

But Jody and the utility man delight in playing jokes on her. The utility man (who performs the duty of mess boy but doesn't like to be called that) tells us how he slipped a hard-boiled egg in among the raw eggs this morning, and Stella grew purple in the face trying to break it over the edge of the frying-pan.

Returning to the pilot-house, we find the captain at the wheel. 'At the wheel' is purely metaphorical, for the steering of the gigantic fleet of barges and towboat is done by slight pressure on a small lever.

The captain's name is E. H. Vorwald, but everyone calls him Guttenberg Mike. Guttenberg is his home town, but why the 'Mike' we never do learn.

Gossiping with him is a veteran riverman, Captain Frank P. McCaffrey, eighty years old, who has piloted almost every type of big craft that has floated on the Mississippi during the last half-century. His reminiscences are filtered through a heavy chew of tobacco and are sometimes not as coherent as they might be. But his aim at the spittoon is still good and his comparisons between the old and new days are vivid.

The two are arguing about steam and diesel. The gist of the argument seems to be that while steam is soft and smooth and sweet, diesel power sometimes shakes the boat so that you think your teeth are going to fall out and the noise can be deafening.

On the other hand, twenty-two men are required on a steamboat, seventeen on a diesel. The diesel has more manoeuvrability. Most important, it's more powerful.

A steam-driven towboat (and there are still a few left on the Mississippi) develops around 2,000 horsepower. Diesel boats of 3,600 and 4,000 horsepower are common. Boats of 6,000 horsepower will be ploughing the river by the time this is printed, and 8,000 horsepower diesels are on the drawing board.

Mike points out that a diesel can push four 100-car train-loads of goods upstream against a strong current at about seven miles an hour, and half again as fast downstream.

In the finest days of the steamboat era a thousand packets were on the river carrying a tonnage of 250,000 tons. Now it would take not a thousand, but only ten diesel towboats to handle that tonnage.

'Yes,' said the veteran, 'but don't forget that the biggest tow ever on the Mississippi – 53,200 tons – was pushed by the *Sprague*, and she was a steamer.'

'True enough, but look at the size of her, more than three hundred feet long, the biggest sternwheeler ever built and as clumsy as a cow. Why, her wheel was fourteen feet across, half of it above the floor of the pilothouse and half below. She never wanted to go around a bend, she didn't back properly, and she required a crew of 35 men.'

So the argument will continue on the Mississippi until there are no more men who remember steam.

The pilot-house is a big glass room. The glass is kept clean and there is an uninterrupted 360-degree view of river and shore. In this room the man at the steering levers, whether the pilot or the captain, is king.

No one enters without his permission. No one speaks unless spoken to. A high degree of concentration is necessary in piloting a big tow down an ever-changing river.

At times the tension lets up and the master settles in his chair on the small of his back, puts his feet up on the controls, and starts a conversation with his guest.

He does not need a guest to have a conversation. Even when he is alone he is not alone. Over his radiophone he chats with the master of some other vessel, perhaps miles away, perhaps just around the next bend but still unseen. It is important that an upcoming and downcoming tow should not take each other by surprise. They compare notes.

'I'm close to the right bank but the current is swinging me out.'

'Okay. I'll hug the sand-bar and give you a wide berth.'

But the talk is not limited to official matters.

'How's that bad tooth of yours? Did you get to a dentist?'

'How could I get to a dentist? No, I just tied it to a door-knob and slammed the door.'

In a dense fog the tow keeps on going. The radar screen shows the river and its shores. When another boat appears on the screen the master picks up his telephone. He cannot see the boat, he cannot even see out to the front end of his tow, but there is the boat on the screen and here is the master's voice coming over the phone. They talk things over, decide what to do, where to pass.

In this respect the modern river boats are far ahead of most ocean-going vessels. Many of the latter are not equipped with telephones for ship-to-ship or ship-to-shore calls. Many sea disasters are due to this lack of easy communication. If the *Andrea Doria* had been able to chat with the captain of the *Stockholm*, the collision that took more than fifty lives might have been avoided. Ocean vessels come up the Mississippi as far as Baton Rouge and are a menace to other shipping when they cannot be reached by the human voice.

The master uses another phone if he wishes to talk to the engine-room. He has still another connected by a wire running out along the barges to the front of the tow. This is called the teletalk or, more commonly, the 'tattletale'.

Time was when the captain would shout through a megaphone to the men on the barges. The second mate would megaphone back. Every word had to be clearly pronounced and sung, not spoken.

As tows became bigger and longer, it did not work so well. With the 'tattletale' there is no need to sing or shout. Words almost whispered are amplified into thunder. Both the teletalk and the radiophone make a mouse a lion. Soft-spoken men have their mildest remarks come out with a roar like the blast of a trumpet.

10

Cities That Never Were

WE PASS A CITY OF DREAMS. With eyes open you see
nothing but a house or two, but if you will close your eyes
you can see many beautiful and busy streets, stores and
warehouses, five church spires springing a hundred feet into
the air, a magnificent courthouse and docks where huge piles
of freight are being loaded on big steamboats.

That was the way the non-existent city of Nininger was
pictured on the beautifully engraved maps circulated in New
York and Boston early in the steamboat era. Copies of the
Nininger *Daily Bugle* described the social events of Nininger,
how Mrs Newbody had entertained fifty guests at her new
residence on Park Avenue – and the name of every guest was
given – how the big drygoods merchant had gone east to buy
his spring stock, how fast new buildings were going up and
property values rising.

Among the advertisements for grocery stores, haberdash-
eries, hardware stores, millinery stores, shoe stores and blacksmith shops and the announcements of services in the churches
and theatrical performances in the auditorium were notices
of lots that might be had for a good price if the buyer was
quick about it.

Every name, every business, the entire city was a product
of pure imagination. The fraud was on so colossal a scale that it
was perfectly convincing. Easterners bought up the whole

prairie for two miles back from the river at ten thousand dollars an acre and more.

The land sharks then disappeared and the few buyers who managed to get through to the Mississippi searched in vain among the sloughs and marshes for the city of Nininger.

Rolling Stone was another such mythical metropolis and dozens of promoters got out glowing prospectuses on imaginary town sites all along the river below St Paul.

* * *

As we near Red Wing the magnificent fling of river and islands and the upthrust of rocky walls that confine the valley need a Mark Twain to describe them. Fortunately we have his description:

> 'The majestic bluffs that overlook the river, along through this region, charm one with the grace and variety of their forms, and the soft beauty of their adornment. The steep, verdant slope, whose base is at the water's edge, is topped by a lofty rampart of broken, turreted rocks, which are exquisitely rich and mellow in color – mainly dark browns and dull greens, but splashed with other tints. And then you have the shining river, winding here and there and yonder, its sweep interrupted at intervals by clusters of wooded islands threaded by silver channels; and you have glimpses of distant villages, asleep upon capes; and of stealthy rafts slipping along in the shade of the forest wall; and of white steamers vanishing around remote points. And it is all as tranquil and reposeful as dreamland, and has nothing this-worldly about it – nothing to hang a fret or a worry upon.'

Red Wing is an attractive town with its picturesque Barn Bluff towering over the river and its unique 'floating city' of boathouses that climb up and down gin poles as the water level rises and falls. Later, when we come down the river by car, we are to stop here to see the famous potteries and the tannery where a hide goes through so many operations that we shall never complain again about the cost of a pair of shoes. It takes thirty days for it to complete the seventy to eighty processes required. It is cured, washed, scalped of its hair, tanned, washed, dried, sliced, rubbed, washed, scraped, sandpapered, stretched, softened, glazed, measured in machine after machine, and every machine costs from ten thousand to forty thousand dollars. The payroll is one and a half million dollars.

And all this does not give you a pair of shoes. It merely conditions the hide which must then go to the shoe factories to be turned into footwear.

Below Red Wing the Mississippi expands to form Lake Pepin, a fine sheet of water some twenty miles long and two wide, bordered on the Wisconsin side by an escarpment four hundred feet high, weatherbeaten into fantastic shapes. One of its picturesque crags is Maiden's Rock from which a Sioux Indian maid is supposed to have leaped to her death rather than marry the warrior selected by her parents.

Many more have gone to their death in Lake Pepin which used to be known as the 'steamboat graveyard' and was purported by oldtimers to be the 'storm kettle of America', the place where all the storms of the country were brewed. Here an excursion boat went down drowning 98 persons, and here when the river was in flood a strong current carried large ice-floes that poured on down the river with a roar of thunder, tearing out bridge piers, pontoon bridges, sheer booms, pilings and icebreakers, and smashed steamboats, boathouses and houseboats.

Onslaughts of ice are less savage now that locks and dams have tamed the river – but a storm on Lake Pepin is still avoided if possible by all boats large and small.

From Red Wing past Lake Pepin and for many miles beyond through what is reminiscently known as the Hiawatha

Valley the road hugs the Mississippi and affords views that can hardly be excelled elsewhere in America.

By boat it is even finer. Between St Paul and St Louis there are more than five hundred islands large enough to have names or at least numbers, and thousands of islets. The river broadens at times to three miles or more. It is a striking fact that in many places the Upper Mississippi is wider than after it has been joined by the Missouri and the Ohio.

Nor is there any monotony in the vegetation of the islands and river walls. Every form and colour is provided by the intermingling of cottonwood, ash, poplar, elm, white birch, black walnut, red cedar, ironwood, juniper, wild apple, hazelnut, elderberry, dogwood and sumac.

Near Alma is a rugged peak looking like the great Sphinx and on the Iowa side is Pike's Peak, named for Zebulon M. Pike before he went on to give his name to another peak in Colorado.

The many locks and dams have converted the river into a staircase of placid lakes full of islands, and these lakes make pleasant cruising grounds for thousands of houseboats.

We sail past Winona but are later to stop there to take a cruise with a houseboat builder named Whittaker and his wife on one of their Whitcrafts. The boat is a cleverly devised floating house consisting of forward deck, roomy cabin, galley, head (toilet), closet, aft cabin with four bunks, rear deck and open deck above. All this in thirty-two feet of length and eleven-foot beam. The boat draws only twenty-two inches and is powered by a 125-horsepower inboard motor. It will do fourteen miles an hour in still water, about seventeen downstream.

The Whitcraft turns in its own length. It does not have to be removed from the water for the winter – it can be allowed to freeze in. The floating house perhaps cannot be expected to be as cheap as a house of the same size on shore. It costs some ten thousand dollars, more if there are frills. Each boat is

The Mormons in their westward hegira paused to build the city of Nauvoo. Its temple, said by Joseph Smith to be "the most magnificent religious edifice in the world," was burned to the ground, leaving little but this capital representing the sun of divine favor and the horns of plenty in the hands of God.

In some stretches the Mississippi is more land than water. Between St. Paul and St. Louis there are 500 sizeable islands and thousands of islets, the retreat of fugitives from justice and adventure-loving Huck Finns. On one was found a hairy "missing link" which turned out to be "the man from Borneo" escaped from a circus.

→

Two immortal figures look down on the storybook town of Hannibal, scene of the exploits of Tom Sawyer and Huck Finn and home of their creator, Mark Twain.

She looks quite capable of pulling out a big one. The Mississippi pad-dlefish is six feet long, the sturgeon is eight feet. The gar, most fero-cious and irritable of all Mississippi fish, stretches to a length of fifteen feet, four feet of which is jaw.

The modern "towboat" is actually a pushboat. In the distant past it did haul its string of barges, which whipped about like a crocodile's tail. Today the barges are put in front instead of behind, and bound to the towboat so firmly with steel cables that the entire fleet becomes a single rigid unit controlled by the least touch on the steering lever in the pilothouse.

The tow (still called a "tow" although it is pushed, not pulled) may consist of two dozen barges stretching a quarter mile ahead of the pilothouse and carrying the load of an American freight train four miles long. To steer this floating three acres between the stone piers of a bridge is no mean task.

The captain makes up a tow. Each block represents one barge. Where each barge will be placed depends upon many factors such as comparative loads, inflammability of the cargo, provision for dropping off certain barges at near ports without disturbing those bound to far ports.

The man at the controls is king. No one enters the wheelhouse without his permission. No one speaks unless spoken to. A high degree of concentration is necessary in piloting a big tow down an ever-changing river.

The master of a towboat has the world at his ear. Over the radiophone he may confer with the masters of unseen vessels hidden behind points or in fog. By another phone he talks to his engineer. By another, called the tattletale, he reaches the lookout at the front end of his tow a quarter mile away. By another he makes connection with land lines and may chat with anyone on the face of the globe who has a telephone.

Though the responsibility is greater than of old, the operation is infinitely easier. Instead of a gigantic wheel sometimes fourteen feet in diameter requiring the brute strength of several men, today a few buttons and levers lightly touched guide an integrated craft longer than the *Queen Elizabeth*.

The engineer runs a power plant delivering up to eight thousand horsepower. In the best days of the steamboat era a thousand packets carried 250,000 tons. Now ten towboats can do the same job.

From the messboy who peels the potatoes to the head chef who smokes a cigar and gives orders, the staff of the towboat kitchen (it is *not* called a galley) prepares mountains of food. The barge lines take a leaf from the book of the oldtime lumber camps where it was thought good policy to feed men well so they could work well.

An amusement park afloat. The great sidewheeler, *Admiral,* is the largest river excursion steamer in the world. The main deck is a water-borne Coney Island, the second is a ballroom accommodating two thousand dancers at one time, two decks are given over to restaurants and the top deck is for those who are not too busy playing games, dancing or eating to look at the scenery.

One of the last of the showboats, the *Goldenrod,* stages a melodrama every night at eight-thirty. Captain J. W. Menke has taken her up and down the Mississippi and every navigable tributary for the past half century.

→

The great iron rings are embedded in the St. Louis waterfront but the steamboats that used to be moored to them are gone. Such craft had a short life expectancy. They seldom lasted four or five years. Sometimes they were destroyed wholesale. Twenty-three steamers went up in flames along this waterfront on the night of May 17, 1849.

Cairo is dangerously placed between the Ohio on the one side and the Mississippi on the other, therefore high concrete levees circle the city. The opening *(right)* can be quickly closed when the floods come. "Channel reports" of the U.S. Corps of Engineers and the Coast Guard are placed in the mail boxes where they are freely available to river captains or anyone concerned with the condition of the river.

custom-made to the buyer's specifications. One was built as
a study for a floating author.

This houseboat builder is beginning construction of a
marina at Winona large enough to accommodate 150 forty-
foot cruisers and houseboats. Still another marina is being
completed among the islands, and the dredger, A. J. Kertzman, uses his sixty-four-foot houseboat as his floating home
and office. This seems to qualify as the biggest houseboat on
the entire Mississippi. Evidently the only thing that stopped
Mr Kertzman at sixty-four feet was the fact that a craft
sixty-five feet or more must carry a pilot. When we boarded
the craft at the dredger's invitation we found its three decks
humming with the excited chatter of thirty Soroptomists
whom the public-spirited Skipper Kertzman was entertaining
on an excursion upriver.

Nowhere over the entire length of the Mississippi was there
such houseboat activity as at Winona. The two new marinas
will give Winona five good harbours in all for her thousands
of small craft.

The river population requires aquatic policemen, and we
rode with a sheriff in a launch bearing on its side in enormous
letters, 'Sheriff's Patrol'. A glimpse of this law-boat doubtless
has the same restraining effect upon the unruly as the
appearance of a police-car on the highway.

This devotion to law is a bit ironical when one recalls that
it was lawlessness, not law, that saved Winona from ex-
tinction.

River traffic was vital to the existence of Winona. The
village grew up around the steamboat-landing and depended
upon the boats for incoming and outgoing trade. But in 1857
the whimsical river cut a new channel several miles away and
left Winona stranded on a backwater. Steamboats followed
the new route and slow death crept over the formerly busy
port.

But the town officials were not to be beaten so easily.

They concocted a scheme worthy of a Machiavelli. They announced plans to build a stone court-house. The contractor under their direction quarried the great blocks of stone from the bluffs on the opposite side of the river and loaded them on a huge barge. When the barge was exactly in the middle of the new channel there was an 'unfortunate accident', the barge upset, and the stone blocked the passage. The river resumed its old course and steamboats once more called at Winona.

*   *   *

Through a paradise of islands in a valley six miles wide between ranges spurred into any number of cliffs to accommodate lovesick Indian maidens, we proceed to a region where the Mississippi actually consists of more land than water, so many are its islands. The Dresbach Dam looms up like a Roman aqueduct.

The lock is not big enough to take our whole tow at one bite. Like most of the Mississippi locks, it is 600 feet long and 110 feet wide. We must resort to double locking – that is, tie off half of the barges to the shore, put the other half through the lock, then come back for the rest. This takes an hour or more, whereas single locking takes fifteen minutes.

'When the locks were built,' says the lockmaster, 'a future of 750,000 tons a year was anticipated. Now seven million tons a year go through, nearly ten times what was expected. Our locks should be at least twice as big as they are. It was too bad we couldn't see ahead, but who could have imagined that Mississippi traffic would make such a comeback?'

In addition to commercial traffic, the number of small boats using the locks has increased amazingly. Every lockmaster would like to have a supplementary small lock to pass small boats. It is very expensive to open a 600-foot lock for a rowboat or a motorboat, but it must be done.

We found the bridge at La Crescent closed and the local newspaper the next day told why.

'Swarms of flies which dwell along the Mississippi River sloughs descended on the bridge early yesterday because someone forgot to turn off the bridge lights.

'Flies landing on the roadway were crushed and caused slippery conditions, wrecking a truck and three autos.

'Two truckloads of sand solved the traction problem, but not before a delay of an hour and a half had piled up lines of traffic three miles on each side of the river.'

The Mississippi is not famous for its bathing beaches and those that exist are none too safe. The ever-changing and always powerful currents have no patience with inexpert swimmers. At Pettibone Beach just over the river from La Crosse we found lifeguards searching the river bottom for the body of a woman drowned an hour before.

She and two companions had been pulled under. There were two lifeguards on duty and they did all that could be expected of them, each saving one bather, but when they returned for the third she was not to be found.

So the river can be a devil even before it has fallen in with its evil companions, the Missouri and Ohio.

*   *   *

What does a *Life* photographer do when he retires? We found out what one of them does – he acts as midwife to expectant dragonflies. We ran into Wallace Kirkland on a La Crosse street and he invited us to his shack in the woods to witness a birth. There we had coffee with him and his wife and tried to keep clear of the tangle of cables, legs of tripods, photographic shooting-irons of all sorts that filled the living-room.

This incidentally was the only room. The shack had been rented for twenty dollars a month and had an outside toilet.

However, it was exactly what the amateur naturalist needed, for it overlooked a pond filled with bugs.

In a glass tank dragonfly nymphs swam about. One of them had climbed out of the water on a grass stem and was strangely silent. Kirkland was watching it day and night, for it was plainly about to shed its dull case and emerge as a brilliant dragonfly. He must have his cameras ready to record the event. He was a man of supreme patience.

'Oh, I've often had to baby-sit with a nymph all night.'

His purpose was to record the entire life-cycle of a dragonfly, then publish the pictures in the *National Geographic Magazine* and perhaps a book.

Several times we rose but he would not allow us to go. 'It will happen any minute now.' He had asked several other friends in for the happy event. They arrived, and waited.

After innumerable cups of coffee, it happened. The dull, ash-brown Cinderella cast aside her cloak and emerged in full technicolour to the tune of a clicking Exakta and a whirring Bolex.

Kirkland beamed. 'Very successful birth,' he said. 'Sometimes I have to do a Caesarean.'

He handed out cigars.

Through island reaches that call back memories of Japan's Inland Sea we journey from thriving La Crosse to historic Prairie du Chien where girls in the costume of a century ago show guests the treasures of Villa Louis. This remarkably civilized home was built on the savage frontier by Hercules Dousman, fur-trader agent for John Jacob Astor.

River roads are rare along the Mississippi, but from Prairie du Chien south there is a beautiful hill road along the west shore of this highly picturesque stretch of river. It is unknown to tourists, since it is not a red-line route, but certainly no finer river views may be had from any other road in America.

The Great River Road is a project for the future. It is to follow the magnificent river from source to mouth. This will take time, for there are many difficulties of terrain to be overcome, cliffs, swamps, sloughs, bayous and levees.

The project was launched by the Federal Aid Highway Act of 1954 authorizing an initial expenditure of a quarter of a million dollars by the Bureau of Public Roads 'for the purpose of expediting the interstate planning and co-ordination of a continuous Great River Road and appurtenances thereto traversing the Mississippi Valley from Canada to the Gulf of Mexico'.

Under this Act the Commissioner of Public Roads has made available to the ten Mississippi River states the services of leading highway engineers and landscape architects experienced in the development of scenic parkways.

At Guttenberg, our skipper, 'Guttenberg Mike', hands up pies baked in the *Huck Finn*'s kitchen (it's not called a galley on riverboats) to members of his family who have come to see his boat pass through the lock. It's hello and good-bye for another month or so. The men of the towboats have little home life.

II

Aboard the Huck Finn

NIGHT AND DAY the towboat ploughs on. It may pause
at a town to put off a barge or take one on and it must halt
at the locks. But ordinarily it slides along with no sound but
that of the engines. There is no bustle on the decks and no
talk except in the pilot-house. You get a weird feeling that it
is a ghost ship going through a No Man's Land. Half the
men are asleep and the other half keep quiet so they can sleep.

Surely unique among the world's hotels is the Green Tree
Hotel on the river front at Le Claire.

For it actually *is* a green tree, a magnificent elm rhapsodized
by Mark Twain and enshrined in the Hall of Fame for Trees
in Washington.

Twice as broad as it is high, shading an area of a hundred
feet in diameter and affording a fine view up and down the
river, it became a rendezvous for penniless rivermen. It
adjoined the steamboat landing and there was no better
place to keep an eye out for a new riverboat job. Under its
shade men spread their blankets and cooked their meals and
made their home for weeks at a time. They dubbed this
inexpensive open-air lodging-house the Green Tree Hotel
and it became known by that name among rivermen from
St Paul to New Orleans.

Among the boys who played beneath the Green Tree was
one who grew up to be a legend for all boys everywhere. He was

a famous scout and guide, a rider for the Pony Express, and a buffalo hunter with a contract to provide meat for the labourers building the Kansas-Pacific Railroad. It was this latter occupation that earned him his nickname. Under the Green Tree stands a granite slab to his memory and it bears this inscription:

Dedicated to
Colonel William F. Cody
'Buffalo Bill'
By his friend and boyhood playmate
Joe Barnes
erected in 1924

The Green Tree Hotel has been open for business since long before the War Between the States, and as we passed we could see that it was still fully booked up, more than fifty men and boys cooking, eating, playing cards or playing pranks in its cool shade.

* * *

Large cities are becoming more numerous, Dubuque, Davenport, Moline, Rock Island, Burlington, Quincy.

Deep in its Mormon memories lies Nauvoo. Here the Saints had come from Missouri when they were expelled from that state because of fear of their ambitions as printed in their *Book of Commandments* in which Missouri was called 'the land of your inheritance, which is now the land of your enemies'.

Mormon missionaries sent converts from other states and even from England to Nauvoo which speedily became a city of twenty thousand people, a greater population than Chicago could boast at that time. Because the Mormons voted in a bloc, the state of Illinois became nervous over its political potentialities, particularly when Joseph Smith announced himself a candidate for president of the United States.

Life was not easy in Nauvoo. The winters were rigorous and the summers malarial. The Mormons had no competent doctors, but their leader, Joseph Smith, practised faith-healing. Brigham Young later recalled the prophet's miracles,

'Joseph commenced in his own house and dooryard, commanding the sick in the name of Jesus Christ to arise and be made whole, and they were healed according to his words. He then continued to travel from house to house, healing the sick as he went.'

These wonders were proclaimed abroad and immigrants streamed in from Europe. They were advised by the missionaries that delay would be fatal since it was God's plan that the Atlantic would dry up and the journey to America would then be impossible. It was said that the holy city enjoyed the special favour of the Lord who rained down manna like wafers dipped in honey in such abundance that no one might go hungry.

Joseph Smith had numerous 'revelations' in one of which he was commanded to build a temple which should be 'the most magnificent religious edifice in the world'. It was built of native white limestone at a cost of a million dollars and combined Romanesque, Greek and Egyptian architecture. Topping its spire was a golden figure of the angel Moroni, he who had revealed to Joseph Smith the golden plates which, translated, became the Book of Mormon.

In another revelation Joseph Smith was directed to establish the doctrine of 'celestial marriage', an exalted term for polygamy. Plural marriage was to be not only permissible but desirable, it being Mormon doctrine that no woman could enter Heaven unless sealed 'for time and eternity' to a member of the Mormon church. Women who might have remained single were thus mated and saved from the fires of Hell.

Not all Mormons supported the new doctrine. Dissenters published a newspaper which in its first issue denounced polygamy and condemned Smith's political aspirations. The first number of this newspaper was the last. The press was smashed, the printing plant burned, the perpetrators stripped of their property, and forced to flee for their lives.

The fugitives entered a complaint with state authorities and a warrant was issued for the arrest of Joseph Smith. The prophet defied the writ and gathered about him a military force called the Nauvoo Legion and declared martial law in Nauvoo.

For these acts, he was charged with treason and transferred to the county gaol in Carthage. Here lynchers broke in upon him. He made a dash for the window and leaped to his death on the stone flags of the gaol yard.

The trek led by Brigham Young from Nauvoo to Utah is history and the fine character of the Mormon community in that state is well known. Nauvoo is a modern river town like many others, now more Catholic than Mormon, but houses of the first settlers are still to be seen and two of them have been turned into museums. The proud temple was destroyed by fire and the stones were carted away to build houses and stables.

*   *   *

Now we come to a recently completed marvel, the new Keokuk Lock, believed by the U.S. Engineers to be the world's largest in water volume. It is 1,200 feet long and 110 wide (Panama locks are 1,000 feet long and 110 wide). Until its completion the lock at Granite City was the longest on the Mississippi. It also was 1,200 feet long and 110 wide, but it has a drop of only a few feet while the normal full depth of the Keokuk Lock is 38·2 feet.

To get a true impression of its size it is necessary to enter it in a small canoe, as I did later, and look up at its towering walls. It was a striking contrast – one of the smallest of boats in the largest of locks. This immense concrete tank, with as much water capacity as a small lake, fills to the level of the upper pool in about ten minutes. The old lock was only 358 feet long. It was a bottleneck. A towboat with an eleven-barge tow could not get through in less than seven hours. Today the same tow would go through in twenty minutes.

*   *   *

The *Huck Finn* 'turns' the *Missouri*. This is a rather extraordinary operation. The two towboats trade tows.

The *Huck Finn* edges over to the shore, the deck-hands throw off the lines that bind the tow to the towboat, and the three-acre raft of barges is tied to a big cottonwood.

Then the *Huck Finn* continues downstream and meets the *Missouri* coming up pushing a big load of oil and sulphur. The *Huck Finn* passes the *Missouri*, turns about and comes up beside her.

While the two boats are cheek by jowl, we step from one to the other, for we wish to continue downstream while the *Huck Finn* returns to Minneapolis.

The *Missouri* has thrown off its connections with its tow. Now it slows its engines and falls away and the *Huck Finn* takes its place behind the fleet and is wired fast.

The tow never knows the difference. Even when there is nothing to push it, its tremendous momentum would keep it moving upstream a half mile before it would notice the current.

The operation is completed when the *Missouri* puts itself behind what was the *Huck Finn*'s tow, wires fast, throws off the mooring from the cottonwood tree and proceeds downstream.

Why the turn? Some towboats are better adapted to the lower reaches, some to the upper. The *Missouri* can cope with strong currents. She has officially 3,600 horsepower and can develop 4,000. She is one of the newer boats and a million dollars could not replace her. Even at that she is not the finest on the Mississippi – the *Haynes*, a still newer boat belonging to another line, cost two million dollars to build.

It is curious that these great craft are not called ships, but the word 'ship' is taboo on the Mississippi. It is as much of a sin to call a boat a ship on the river as to call a ship a boat at sea.

We are taken up to our quarters. Here is towboat luxury indeed. Our cabin is without exception the largest and most luxurious we have ever had on any boat or ship anywhere in the world in some forty years of travel.

Thirty-two feet long and sixteen wide, its big windows look out to the right shore and to the left and full ahead, its walls are wood-panelled and its ceiling and floor parqueted, two air-conditioning units give it any climate desired, there is enough furniture to equip a hotel lobby, and its private bath alone is as large as an average cabin on the *Queen Elizabeth*.

It is customary to provide a room of this sort on every towboat for the convenience of travelling officials of the company. If the room does not happen to be so occupied it may be available to outsiders who have some special interest in the river.

We are called to the pilot-house to meet Captain Marks. As he talks he nonchalantly glances at the river now and then, flips levers and punches buttons. Directly under his control are the boat's four engines, four propellers, ten rudders (four forward, six for backing), two searchlights, fathometer, radarscope, RCA radio-telephone, Bell System mobile phone by which any number in the world can be called, phone to the engine-room, phone to the tow, gyro-compass which can be set to hold the course without manual control, radio receiver for regular radio programmes, ice water dispenser, and a boy to keep the coffee coming.

*   *   *

We come to storied Hannibal, scene of the exploits of Tom

Sawyer and Huck Finn and home of their creator, Mark Twain.

What was a small village in Twain's day is now a sprawling city, but it still has a sleepy, storybook air and is obviously proud of its Twain tradition. A museum contains many interesting objects associated with the author, and adjoining it is the Clemens home with small rooms, low ceilings, a ladderlike stairway, a severe simplicity revealing the slender means of the family.

A block away down a disreputable alley lived Tom Blankenship, bosom friend of young Sam Clemens. At night the boys would converse from one house to the other by means of a code of catcalls. Then Sam would step out the window, slide down the roof of the house and descend by an arbour to join his arch conspirator for a night of mischief. Of course Tom Blankenship was the ideal prototype for Huck Finn.

Near by is Wildcat Corner where in Selm's store Huck sold a coonskin to the proprietor for ten cents. It was tossed on a pile of furs at the back of the store. Sam climbed through an open window retrieved the skin and returned it to Tom who went into the store and sold it for another ten cents. This was continued until the plot was discovered.

At the foot of Cardiff Hill we came upon Tom Sawyer and Huck Finn in person. The bronze figures are splendidly done to represent the carefree dress and adventurous spirit of two boys who somehow seem more real to young readers than many of their own living friends.

They are real because they are drawn from life and many of the incidents as written were exactly as lived by Sam Clemens and Tom Blankenship. Becky Thatcher also was no fiction. Her actual name was Laura Hawkins. She later married a Doctor Frazer. In 1926 Harold Speakman talked with Mrs Frazer and reported the interview in *Mostly Mississippi*:

" 'Will you tell us some of the things you remember about Mark Twain?'

" 'Well, Mr Clemens and I went to the same school, you know. Samuel was just an ordinary boy, very average, and didn't show much ability of any kind. He had a habit of telling stories in a slow drawling voice that somehow made you listen. They weren't very good stories. If anyone else had told them, they wouldn't have amounted to anything; but when Samuel told them, they usually sounded quite funny. He had no gift of writing, as far as any of us knew. He used to get into scrapes quite a lot, and he often played hookey from school, but he was a nice boy and used to divide his candy and oranges with me. Like a great many other American boys, he had his pockets filled with queer things to trade." '

" 'And you first met him as he tells about it in *Tom Sawyer*?'

" 'Yes. Pretty much that way. The first meeting was when Samuel turned handsprings in front of our house, and accidentally struck me on the head. Then we became acquainted. A great many years later, he invited my granddaughter and me to his home in Connecticut. It was a fine visit." '

She brought out a photograph of Samuel Clemens which he had given her shortly before his death. On it was written, 'To Laura Frazer, from her earliest sweetheart.'

We poked our way into McDougal's Cave where Tom Sawyer and Becky Thatcher got lost, repeating more or less the actual experience of Sam Clemens and Laura Hawkins. It was and is a bewildering labyrinth of tunnels, rifts and chasms, some of the passageways believed to penetrate beneath the Mississippi itself. There have been many weird goings-on here. It was a hiding place for runaway slaves, and a refuge for criminals. A St Louis doctor with a macabre passion for scientific inquiry placed a girl's body in a remote chamber among the stalactites to see if it would petrify.

South of the town is Lover's Leap whose legend of Indian

lovers going to their death is not as interesting as the actual record of what happened here in the 1840s, when a religious group selected this as a jumping-off place to Heaven.

Their leader, a New York deist, had warned them that the end of the world was at hand. Thousands were convinced. They resigned their jobs, neglected their crops, closed their stores, dressed in long white robes and ascended to the pinnacle to await the final trump. It did not come.

The deist explained the reason – lack of faith. Some doubters had failed to surrender their earthly possessions. They would have one more chance. He himself would accept their earthly goods, thus freeing their souls for the great event which was now scheduled to take place on 22 October of the following year.

The faithful divested themselves of all but their white robes, ascended once more to the crest above the winding Mississippi, and again Gabriel was silent. The dispossessed looked for the deist, but he was not to be found.

Sam Clemens became a printer's devil on a small Hannibal newspaper and later an assistant editor. He enlivened the paper with spicy personal articles, some of them rather explosive. One of his productions was a poem titled, 'To Miss Katie of Hannibal.' Unluckily the title was too long for the column, therefore in an unguarded moment he abbreviated it to read, 'To Miss Katie of H—l.' He wrote later, 'For once the Hannibal *Journal* was in demand and actually booked the unparalleled number of thirty-three subscribers.'

The river was his joy and his love. He stowed away on a packet, was discovered, and thrown ashore nine miles downstream. He studied for a pilot's licence, got it, and came to know intimately every island and bend from St Paul to New Orleans.

Late in life he returned to Hannibal and climbed the hill to get a comprehensive view.

'The whole town lay spread out below me then, and I could

mark and fix every locality, every detail. Naturally, I was a good deal moved. I said, "Many of the people I once knew in this tranquil refuge of my childhood are now in Heaven; some, I trust, are in the other place." '

'A month ago,' says the captain as we lie in Lock 23, 'a man was killed here. An empty petrol barge exploded. They think the spark that set it off must have been caused by the friction of a rope against the lock wall.'

'But how could a petrol barge explode if it was empty?'

'An empty one is more dangerous than a full one. The liquid is comparatively stable but after it has been taken out the tank fills up with gas. If there is a leak, all you need is a spark to have an explosion.'

We pass a large wooded island.

'That's where they caught the wild man,' the captain says. 'People on the mainland noticed something moving on the island. They thought it might be a cow that had somehow got stranded there. The sheriff went over to investigate. He caught sight of a hairy creature but couldn't tell what it was. It looked like a hyena. But it was eating grass, and hyenas don't. He didn't care to tackle it singlehanded so he came back for help. He took some men along and captured the thing. It was "the man from Borneo" escaped from a circus. The circus was very glad to get him back.'

On the right bank is Portage des Sioux which has its own romantic story. In the floods of 1951 the town was threatened by the rising river. The people, French Catholics, prayed that the town be spared. At the last minute the waters subsided. In gratitude, a tall white statue of the Madonna has been erected. It is called Our Lady of the Rivers and is probably unique among madonnas since it is made of reinforced fibreglass. It rises twenty-six feet high on a seventeen-foot pedestal and is illuminated at night as a guide for river traffic.

The great Missouri ends its long journey from Saskatchewan,

Montana and Wyoming through North Dakota, South Dakota, Nebraska, Iowa, Kansas and Missouri and pays tribute to the Father of Waters in the form of millions of tons of the mid-west's most fertile soil. The Mississippi at first refuses to accept the gift and the two tides, one black and one brown, flow side by side with little intermingling. Gradually infiltration takes place and the Mississippi will never be itself again until it drops its dirt load at the Gulf.

It is interesting to speculate what would have happened if the American continent had been explored from the west rather than from the east. In that case the Mississippi might now be considered the longest river in the world. The explorers would have come first upon the western river and the stream now known as the Upper Mississippi would have been put down as merely one of the great river's many tributaries. Certainly at the junction the stream from the north is far less impressive than the Missouri.

12

Playboat and Showboat

WE DISEMBARK AT ST LOUIS, which used to see a
hundred steamboats lined up along her jetty at one time and
which now knows an amount of river traffic never dreamed of
in steamboat days.

But there is one remarkable and thriving survival of the
old days – the steamboat, *Admiral*. We go aboard her for an
afternoon excursion.

It is a truly fabulous boat, the biggest river excursion
steamer in the world, 387 feet long, six decks high, 98 feet
from the water to the top of the pilot-house.

It was built shortly after the turn of the century at Vicksburg
as a railroad ferry. It was made over into an excursion boat
in 1941 – and what a face-lifting!

One of its main features is an enormous ballroom extending
the full length of the boat and accommodating two thousand
dancers at one time. A twelve-piece orchestra provides the
music. Looking down on the dance floor, is a spectators'
gallery, also full boat-length.

The main deck is unbelievable. It is a floating carnival,
a water-borne Coney Island, with every sort of bright and
gaudy machine to play games on, painted horses for the
kiddies, rifle ranges where grizzly bears taunt sharpshooters,
fortune-tellers, ice cream, hot dogs. Even the two huge
connecting rods that turn the great sidewheels are decorated

in bright colours and named Wimpy and Popeye. This amusement park afloat (where railroad trains used to be carried) is as long as a city block and half as wide.

The *Admiral* has been on *Cinerama*, and no wonder, for it is a wonder.

Three of the decks are restaurant decks and the amount of food sold must be stupendous. The fare for the all-afternoon ride is one dollar. Dancing on the great floor is free.

The capacity of the boat is four thousand and on the day of our excursion it was completely sold out. Never have I seen such activity on any boat, such fun-making and food-stowing, so many bulbs flashing, such chattering of women and screeching of happy youngsters, such running about, such prancing to lively music. Passengers on the open upper deck paid some attention to the view. On all other decks everybody was looking in, not out.

The Mississippi has been largely given over to cargo traffic. The success of the *Admiral* is dramatic proof that there is still a place for at least a few of the great pleasure boats that once adorned the river. Long may the steam hiss from her boilers and her great sidewheels churn.

Moored to the St Louis jetty near the *Admiral* is the *Goldenrod*, one of the last of the showboats. She still stages a melodrama every night at 8.30. The bill is changed once every two weeks. Captain J. W. Menke, a sweet and salty old soul with a most infectious grin, has taken her up and down every navigable river of the West. The boat dates back half a century.

We went early to have time to talk to the captain before the show began. The theatre, he said, will seat five hundred downstairs, 480 on the second floor. Audiences now are very small, despite the million population of St Louis. He showed us on the walls of his office pictures of former actors on the *Goldenrod* stage including Red Skelton – and visitors, Will Rogers, Helen Morgan, Irene Dunne, Talullah Bankhead.

Edna Ferber, before she wrote *Show Boat*, wired for a list of his routings. He didn't know who Edna Ferber was and didn't bother to reply. The telegram lay in an accumulation of papers. But when *Show Boat* was brought to his attention he fished out the telegram, framed it, and it now has a permanent place on the wall.

The *Goldenrod* and her captain have known many odd adventures. One of the most curious occurred when the boat, backing away from the wharf, struck a piling which stove in the hull. The captain ran down with a flashlight and discovered a hole as big as a man's body. The boat was bound to sink in a few minutes unless something was done at once. Perhaps it was the story of the Dutch boy with his finger in the dyke that gave Captain Menke an idea and saved his boat.

He dropped into the hole up to his stomach and since his midriff was of generous proportions the fit was perfect. For hours he plugged that hole while the crew worked to bring the boat around and beach her at just the right tilt on the cobbled waterfront so that when the human plug was removed she would not roll over and sink.

The month was February. The river was full of floating ice and the water bitterly cold. Every time the captain began to shiver he was dosed with another slug of whisky or coffee. It was morning before the boat was landed and the captain could be hauled out. But the large and pliable midriff had done its work. Not more than a quart of water had got by.

'When they pulled me out I popped, just like the cork in a bottle of champagne.'

Melodrama is the dish in the old showboats. The play we saw was *Her Legal Prisoner*. The beautiful maiden was, of course, pursued by two men, one a hero and the other a villain. There was an old colonel too. He forgot his lines and after a moment of gasping struggle to remember them, he clutched his neck and said, 'Something wrong with my throat.' That sent both him and the hero into a fit of the titters so that they had to leave the stage.

Between acts a strong-armed musician ripped the intestines
out of an ancient upright.

The best seats were seventy-five cents. The *Goldenrod* is
not making money. Those who wish to see a genuine old
showboat still in action should go soon.

The *Goldenrod* is not the only showboat still to be found on the
Mississippi. At Grand Rapids, Minnesota, we had seen the
Mississippi Melodie come round the bend, crowded to the
gunwhales with actors, the band playing on the foredeck and
the sternwheel throwing spray against the sinking sun.

It is not an old boat but contrived in the old style and
maintained as a community project.

On the dock the townsfolk, dressed in century-old costumes,
hailed its approach. There were wooden seats behind the
dock for the audience. Seventy players made up the cast.
The boat drew up to the dock, the band and the stars disembarked, and the show was on – a variety performance with
singing, dancing, comedy skits. The cast included three very
fine singers.

It is a lovely setting for a little theatre – the hillside among
trees, the dock and boat, the river and sunset-lit shore beyond.
Four performances are given each summer.

And we would later visit the giant *Sprague* tied up to the
shore at Vicksburg. There we met the physician, Dr Walter
Johnston, a hearty fellow active in all community projects
who has been playing the part of a nineteen-year-old for many
seasons in the showboat production, *Gold in the Hills*, on
board the *Sprague*. The character he enacted was a nit-wit.

One night a woman in the audience found herself on the
point of delivering a baby and called,

'Is there a doctor in the house?' The show stopped, people
chattered, and one cried,

'There's one, on the stage.'

'Oh no, not him,' the woman retorted. 'Anybody who could
act such a fool couldn't be a good doctor.'

And on the subject of deliveries Dr Johnston had an amusing anecdote to tell about the time when he and members of his clinic were about to take off on a boat ride and picnic.

All the baskets were packed, everyone was ready to go. Came a phone call – a woman thought her time had come. Was the long-anticipated party to be spoiled?

The doctor said, 'Come down. You're going on a picnic with us.'

Unlike the lady of the showboat, she showed remarkable confidence in her physician. She came. The doctor took along his satchel with everything necessary for delivery. The party was saved. Her time didn't come until a day or so later.

Already gone is the circusboat, gaily painted, carrying a menagerie of ponies, dogs, wildcats, monkeys, a few yards of sluggish serpent, some clowns and acrobats, and a brass band. The amphitheatre of the *Floating Palace* could seat a thousand persons to view bareback riding, trapeze acrobatics, and the growling performance of a mangy lion. The crowds could not be accommodated. Those who could not get in paid a dollar for the privilege of standing on the gunwhale and looking in through the windows.

Then there was the *Banjo* with a troupe of French Zouaves. And the *Romance Wonderland* went up and down the river for thirty years producing thrillers propounding the doctrine that sin, no matter how attractive, must always yield to virtue.

*   *   *

Any historian curious about the steamboat era should visit the home of Captain Donald T. Wright, publisher of *The Waterways Journal* in St Louis. A former river pilot, he has made a priceless collection of steamboat photographs and relics, stored in every cupboard and closet and chest of drawers in every room of the great house, including not only the living-rooms, dining-room and den, but every bedroom and the bathrooms as well. He is loyal to steam. 'It will come back,' he said.

Close to the swift brown Mississippi surging beneath Veterans Memorial Bridge at St Louis is the Eagle Boat Store, probably the oldest boat store on the river. Its business is to supply everything that a steamboat or a towboat may need.

Here we saw great stores of steel cables, ropes, hose, ratchets, lifejackets, running lights, searchlight carbons, shackles, boathooks, machine parts, planks, lanterns, fire extinguishers, electrical items, oil, ladders, oars, outboard motors, groceries of every sort, brooms, mops, soap, hot water bottles, towels and toothpicks.

How are deliveries made? The Boat Store runs a store boat. Let's say that a towboat is coming downriver. Its captain phones his order to the boat store. The supplies are put on the store boat which goes out to meet the towboat.

The towboat does not stop nor even slow down. A boat with an operating expense of several hundred dollars an hour cannot afford to stop for supplies. The towboat ploughs along at full speed while the store boat comes alongside, ties on, chucks the supplies on board, casts off, and returns to port.

The store boat is a small cabin launch and riding along with the monster may be risky because of strong currents or the wash from other tows. The rail may be smashed, the boat may be stove in, it may even be tossed up on the towboat's main deck. A man unloading may be jarred overboard and caught between the two boats. If he escapes the propeller of the small boat he is quite likely to be sucked in under the towboat and minced by its big screws.

We went out on the store boat to regain the *Missouri* which after a trip upriver was now about to repass St Louis. It was nearly midnight. The reflections from the lights on the bridges swirled and tossed in the strong current. We dodged floating logs. Some we could not dodge thundered under the boat to the dire peril of the propeller.

The skipper pointed out a searchlight playing far upriver. 'That's the *Missouri.*' He took down the phone and talked with the captain of the '*Mo*'.

As the two boats approached, we were told when and where to come alongside. This we tried to do gently, but a wayward current flung us against the big boat with a resounding crash.

There was no ceremony about our embarkation – the store boat was anxious to get out of danger. We were fairly thrown aboard the '*Mo*' together with our bags and some boxes and cans of supplies, and the store boat pulled away.

* * *

And so on down the magnificent waterway past the once gay and gaudy and now quite respectable Ste Genevieve, past Cape Girardeau on the Trail of Tears, by which the Cherokees, after being evacuated from their land in Tennessee and Georgia, made their long journey to the unknown west.

We landed in Cairo. Flying back to St Paul, we recovered our car and trailer and spent many days driving down slowly through river towns back to Cairo.

13

Cairo is in Egypt

THIS SOUTHERN END of Illinois is popularly known as Egypt. The reason is not immediately apparent. We see no minarets as we walk up the main street of Cairo (here pronounced Care-oh). Nor are there any temples in nearby Thebes. Nor anything particularly oriental in Orient. We see no hieroglyphic inscriptions in Karnak and neighbouring towns although there are many signs advertising such enterprises as the Egyptian Ironworks, Egyptian Sales Agency, Pyramid Roofing and Lumber Company, Greater Egypt Association, and so on.

How did Southern Illinois become Egypt? It seems to have begun with the naming of Cairo, whose founders considered the location similar to that of the city on the Nile.

Another theory, which does not quite preclude the first, is that, in the early years when there was famine in the upper half of the state, the settlers journeyed down to this fertile country for food as did the Israelites of old to Egypt.

'In the summer of 1824,' wrote a settler, John Comegys, 'there was not a bushel of corn to be had in central Illinois. My father settled that year in Springfield. We had to live there for a time on venison, blackberries and milk while the men were gone to Egypt to harvest and procure breadstuffs.'

There is something faintly tropical about Cairo with its ginkgo trees, magnolias, canebreaks, cotton patches and catfish – and fine old mansions, one of which, the Rendleman House, is now being converted into a museum of steamboat relics and folklore.

Cairo was a slum built in a swamp. Charles Dickens, suffering from indigestion, described it as 'a breeding place of fever, ague and death, a dismal swamp on which the half-built houses rot away, the hateful Mississippi circling and eddying before it and turning off upon its southern course, a slimy monster hideous to behold'.

The visitor to Cairo today would not recognize it by this description. The water has been pumped out of it, most of the mosquitoes banished, and it is as pert and prosperous a town as any other. It is the proud county seat and the serpent that helped make it so deserves a place in history.

Before the turn of the century Thebes was the county seat. But Cairo was ambitious to acquire that honour. There was to be an election for members of the legislature, and a hot contest took place between the Cairo man and a man of Thebes. If the former could be elected there was a very good chance that the county seat might be transferred to Cairo.

An imaginative Cairoene conceived a plan to keep the voters of Thebes away from the ballot box. He wrapped a boulder in a hide, harnessed a mule to it and night after night led the mule through the countryside. The boulder obliterated both his tracks and the mule's, leaving only a smooth depression about four feet wide that could easily be imagined to have been made by a huge serpent.

Presently a woman reported that she had seen a great snake. Then two men claimed that they had seen an enormous serpent five miles above Cairo. Meanderings of the serpent took first-page space in the newspapers. Every morning there was a new track and brave hunters followed it, but it always ended in water. When anyone missed a calf or a hog the loss was blamed on the serpent.

All this took place in the environs of Cairo. Thebes was

some twenty five-miles away by a twisting dirt road. That was a great distance in those days of the horse and buggy. Nevertheless visitors streamed in from Thebes and even more remote points to see the track of the great serpent.

Then it was announced that on a certain day, which just happened to be election day, a grand hunt would be staged for the capture of the serpent. Eager hunters flocked in from points near and far, including Thebes. This was more fun than voting. The crowds were divided into squads and started to scour the country. They came back to the rendezvous to eat at noon and night and the city of Cairo generously provided them with an abundance of food and whisky. It was a hilarious party.

Outsiders failed to notice that Cairo folk disappeared one by one, later returning to the party. The truth is that the city fathers were seeing to it that all Cairo voters got to the polls. Thebans, if they had any qualms of conscience, were much too far from their precincts to get home in time to vote.

The sobering realization came the next day when the votes were counted. The Cairo man was elected. The proud Court House in Cairo's main street testifies that this city is now Alexander County's 'seat of justice', and Thebans still squirm over the 'injustice' of it.

Cairo, like Manhattan, is long and narrow and wedged in between two rivers – far greater rivers than those that pass New York. High levees keep out the Mississippi on the one side and the Ohio on the other.

We drove down to the point where the two rivers meet. Walking out to the tip of the land, we had the dark translucent Ohio within ten feet of us on the left, the brown opaque Mississippi equally close on our right. Stretching out ahead of us was a smooth, ripple-free band caused by the boiling of the meeting currents.

In the middle is point zero. For here is where the Upper Mississippi ends and the Lower Mississippi begins. Mileage is counted from this point upstream. Where we stand a marker indicated that we are at 0·8 upriver.

According to our U.S. Engineers map that point in mid-stream, which is zero for the upper river, is 964 for the lower river. This mileage is calculated from Head of Passes where the river, nearing the sea, divides into a number of passes which carry its waters out across the swamps to the Gulf of Mexico. The longest of these is twenty-mile Southwest Pass. Thus the extreme length of the Lower Mississippi is 984 miles.

The Mississippi's delta, geologically speaking, begins at Cairo. Ages ago the Gulf of Mexico penetrated to this point. The mighty river gradually filled it with silt, and now winds nearly a thousand miles through land of its own making.

The Ohio, though shorter than the Missouri, contributes a far greater volume than either the Missouri or the Upper Mississippi itself.

The consequence is that from here on we have a quite different Mississippi. It is no longer a sweet river; it is grand. It is no longer pretty; it is majestic. It has lost its friendliness; now it is to be feared rather than loved.

It is erratic, power-crazy, a half-tamed giant capable of carrying enormous commerce to man's benefit, but guilty of devastating floods, savage eccentricities, sinkings and drownings without number.

It is no longer a small-boat river. Except for two or three hazardous experiments, we leave our little aluminium egg-shell safely on top of the car until we reach the quiet bayous of the South.

But, full of menace though it may be, the Lower Mississippi is the most significant river on the planet in the value of its cargoes, and one of the most exciting to the traveller.

14

A River Changes Its Sex

THE MISSISSIPPI changes its sex at Cairo. The charming upper river is unmistakably feminine. The big brute of a lower river is just as certainly masculine.

It was on these lower reaches that the Indian and Negro nicknames, Old Big Strong, Old Man River and Old Devil River were born.

The modest river hiding within its walls becomes a brazen exhibitionist riding on top of the world. The river of the valley is kind to pleasure-seekers and picnickers. The river of the sky bears the bulk of the commercial traffic. Although some of the big tows press through to Minneapolis, many stop at St Louis and a great number are diverted up the Ohio.

On the upper river the superstitious say that you can see the ghosts of the lovelorn Indian maidens who leaped from cliffs. But the great mythical figure of the lower river is not a maiden. It is Old Al, the River King.

Old Al was created by the black roustabouts of the steamboat age, but even the modern deckhands of the towboats sometimes declare that they have seen him. As described by folklorist Ben Lucien Burman, Old Al is a male alligator bigger than a barge. He bears a gold crown on his head and holds a huge pipe of tobacco in one of his scaly paws. With his other paw he takes delight in scooping up a sandbar to block a passage or plucking men off barges for his dinner.

With his tail he switches currents this way and that to throw
a tow up against a bridge pier or smash a levee or toss floods
over farms and villages.

The voodoo doctors of the deep South sell good luck charms
guaranteed to keep Old Al in his place. The roustabouts used
to find that a dog or pig dropped overboard would sometimes
mollify the king. And when they became weary loading and
unloading cotton bales they would furtively drop some
tobacco into the water. For it was well known that when Old
Al smoked his pipe the fumes rose from the water and made a
dense fog. This brought the radarless steamboat to a halt
and the roustabouts could rest.

The majesty of the Lower Mississippi is best previewed from
the air. From a small plane we look down on Cairo protected
by high levees from the Ohio on one side and the Mississippi
on the other. Two bridges cross the Ohio from Cairo to
Kentucky, and another spans the Mississippi to the state of
Missouri. Off the point where the two rivers meet the line of
intermingling is plain.

The combined rivers bearing contributions all the way
from Pennsylvania to Montana roll away to the south
through nearly a thousand miles of river-made delta to the
Gulf.

The river behind us is a dug-out river. It has made a trench
for itself and the rock walls of the trench rise sometimes
three hundred feet high.

The river ahead of us has an entirely different idea. It
rides on top of the land, somewhat like an aqueduct.

You look down upon the upper river from the precipices
that contain it. You look up to the lower river from lands that
have to be protected from it by levees.

Streams flow into the upper river. Streams flow out of
the lower river. There are exceptions. One large river, the
Arkansas, and a few smaller ones do manage to penetrate into
the Lower Mississippi. But the mighty Red River, after

coming within seven miles of the Mississippi, gives up the struggle and takes a short-cut to the Gulf.

The farmers of lands from Cairo to the sea are ever conscious of the river above their heads. They are protected by earthen levees thirty to fifty feet high extending for more than 3,500 miles along the main stem and subordinate waterways. This quite eclipses the Great Wall of China, some 1,500 miles long and twenty-two feet high.

Cities are fewer than along the upper river and must choose their sites with care. Vicksburg and Natchez find refuge on hills. New Orleans is normally four to seven feet below river level, in flood time eighteen to twenty feet below. During high water residents may see boats float by above their heads. Rainfall in the city does not drain down and away. It must be pumped *up* into the river.

*   *   *

Sometimes by boat, sometimes by road, we worked our way south. The river bore out a *voyageur*'s description of it – 'a wild, furious, whirling stream'.

We came to New Madrid, a town that has had to move four times to escape the caprices of Old Al, the god-alligator.

We asked someone on the street for the mayor's office. He referred us to a filling station. It bore the name, Tom Hunter. There we were told that Mayor Tom Hunter was downtown getting a haircut. We were asked to wait in the adjoining insurance office.

On its window we noticed the name Shap Hunter. Presently a girl came in and seated herself at a desk. She introduced herself – another Hunter, daughter of Tom.

At last the mayor returned and expressed the opinion that the person who could tell us most about New Madrid was Sam Hunter Jr.

We went to see Banker Sam. He led us to the home of

another Hunter, his Aunt Laura, and she really overflowed with historical data, supplemented a little later by Sam Hunter Sr, and a number of sons and grandsons. We began to wonder if there were any non-Hunters among the 2,800 inhabitants of New Madrid.

It was intended that this should be the capital of a new Spanish empire. Hence the name, New Madrid. It was to be a utopia, the most beautiful city in America, with streets ninety feet wide, parks along the river front, churches of every creed, and no taxes!

In 1811 the river exploded into fountains and geysers thrown up by a violent earthquake. Great waves charged up into the town, bearing boats, crashing into the houses and washing away the lovely riverfront park. Familiar islands disappeared and new ones were thrown up.

The Mississippi, forced back by an upheaval downstream, reversed its course and for several hours flowed north. On the Tennessee side of the river the land sank and the Mississippi flowed into the depression forming what is now known as Reelfoot Lake, eighteen miles long.

The quakes continued for two years. Many of the Utopians abandoned their town, some were granted land in other parts of the state. A band of religious zealots, the Fanatical Pilgrims, announced the end of the world.

This was only the first of a number of river disasters. Four times in all, New Madrid gathered up her skirts and moved back. The site of the original New Madrid is now under the Mississippi River near the Kentucky shore.

'All the buildings on the river,' said Mrs Hunter, 'were kept on rollers during my girlhood. Their owners kept rolling them back.'

New Madrid has now become something of a utopia after all and a more pleasant and livable town would be hard to find. It no longer fears the river since the U.S. Engineers put in dykes upstream causing a bar to form, which diverts the main channel to the Kentucky side. This seemed a good idea at the time. But now that the town, like most others, wants to take advantage of the new traffic on the river and attract industrial plants to New Madrid, it has petitioned the Mississippi River Commission to take measures to change the direction of flow so that the bar will be washed out and New Madrid will have access to a deep-water port for her hoped-for industries.

*   *   *

With Tennessee on one side of us and Arkansas on the other, we feel we are getting into the real South. There is a delicious languor in the air, a sense of relaxation, the opiate of flowering trees and sultry heat.

But if the Northerner supposes his city to be more brisk and crisp than the towns of the Old South, he will be amazed by Memphis. Here is a city as clean and new as a freshly-minted silver dollar. Its dozens of fine old homes are almost lost among the thousands upon thousands of fine new homes representing the best in ultra-modern architecture. Few cities in the nation are growing more rapidly or more tastefully.

Memphis had a bad start. It was plagued by deadly scourges, smallpox, cholera, malaria, dengue and yellow fever. It was more like an enormous garbage dump than a city. The Memphis *Ledger* described the streets as 'huge depots of filth, cavernous Augean stables with no Alpheus to flow through and cleanse them.'

When a yellow-fever epidemic crept up the river from New Orleans in 1878 it took hold with special virulence in Memphis. All who could fled to the country. The rest stayed indoors. Trade and traffic stopped. The stillness was broken only by the cry, 'Bring out your dead,' as the hearses made their rounds. Pits were dug and filled with thousands of corpses.

Devoted doctors and priests did what they could. Women

nursed the sick until they themselves were taken. Even the notorious Annie Cook dismissed her prostitutes and opened her house of ill-fame to yellow fever patients. She herself made beds and carried buckets. The sickness got her and a week later she was dead. The *Appeal* carried this tribute:

'Annie Cook, the woman who after a long life of shame ventured all she had of life and property for the sick, died September eleventh of yellow fever which she contracted while nursing her patients. If there was virtue in the faith of the woman who but touched the hem of the garment of the Divine Redeemer, surely the sins of this woman must be forgiven her.'

Another red-light mistress refused to open her house to the sick; presently she herself became ill and there were those who said it was exactly what she deserved. But she recovered!

There were bizarre and almost comic incidents. In St Patrick's Cathedral solemn mass was held for an important Irish citizen. The service had just got under way when he sat up suddenly in his coffin and demanded,

'What the devil are you doing?'

The epidemic ended with an October frost. Of the 45,000 Memphians, 25,000 had fled, 17,000 had been stricken and 3,000 had died.

It set Memphis back on its heels for half a century. Today there are no visible marks of the painful past. And the discovery in 1900 that yellow fever is transmitted by the little winged messenger of death, the *Aëdes aegypti*, ensured that this chapter in the town's history would not be repeated.

Modern Memphis claims many superlatives. It is the largest cotton market in the world. It is the world's largest hardwood lumber market. It is one of the finest of river ports. President's Island, connected by a causeway to the Memphis mainland, is the largest island in the Mississippi.

John Overton bought the original site of Memphis for ten cents an acre. Recently less than one fifth of an acre in the downtown area was sold for $675,999.

But Cindy, my seventeen-year-old cousin graduating from a Memphis high school, pointed out the really important thing about her city. It is the rock and roll capital of the world.

Elvis Presley, born in Mississippi, went to high school in Memphis and made his home here. Pat Boone is a Tennessee resident. Going back a bit, it was on famous Beale Street, centre of Negro life in Memphis, that the blues were born. Here W. C. Handy wrote *The Memphis Blues* and *The Beale Street Blues*.

Cindy interviewed Elvis Presley for her school paper.

'He was very nice, humble and natural. It was hard to say which one of us was doing the interviewing. He asked me so many questions about me and my school. He doesn't drink or smoke and is good to his parents. He bought a farm for them.'

Memphis is the scene of the annual Cotton Carnival. It is a brilliant affair with its King and Queen and Royal Court, its Royal Barge, its fireworks, its dazzling parties in the halls of the Secret Societies, its three great parades each with a dozen to fifty floats and sixty fine bands.

Race relations are not as tense here as they are across the river in Arkansas. Yet segregation is strictly observed in Memphis buses. 'Front seats are for white persons' is the warning sign near the driver's seat.

All, black and white, must enter by the front door and are equal until they have paid their fares – then the black must proceed to the rear, a difficult matter when the bus is solidly packed in the aisle with standing passengers.

One day we heard a shrill female voice calling to the driver,

'Make this woman sit back. I've told her three times and she won't do it.'

The driver stopped the bus and peered back over the heads

of the standees. In the extreme rear were several empty seats. In front of them on one side sat a coloured girl.

'Sit farther back,' commanded the driver.

She answered, 'I've got a little girl with me.'

The driver craned his neck. Sure enough a small white child sat beside the coloured girl who was evidently a nurse or maid.

'In that case it's all right,' said the driver.

He turned his attention to the other side of the bus. There two coloured women sat in the last seat but one. The driver said,

'You with the flowers in your hat, and the one beside you – move back one seat.'

The two coloured women reluctantly obeyed. Then the white woman who had complained sat down in the seat vacated. It was quite all right to sit where a coloured person had sat, but unthinkable to sit behind one. No one seemed to mind the fact that the incident had held up the bus for five minutes.

Of course the same squeamishness can be found here and there in the North and would be much more noticeable if the Negro population were proportionately as large as in the South. We must leave our own land to get a broader perspective on race. One of the greatest benefits that Americans derive from foreign travel is the discovery that in many other lands the phrase 'all men are created equal', here so often repeated, is there believed.

15

The Shantyboat

SHANTYBOATS used to be numerous on the lower river. There are only a few left. A shantyboat is not quite a houseboat. The difference is that a houseboat is generally used only for an occasional excursion or picnic by a family who can afford such luxury, while a shantyboat is the all-year-round home of a family who can afford nothing better.

The shantyboaters are water gipsies. Once they numbered about thirty thousand. Planks and packing crates floating down the river give them material to build or repair their shanties. They like to put on a porch behind, where they can sit and fish and chew tobacco.

Most of them are English-Irish and have the love of adventure of both breeds. They like the life because it gives them the outdoors, and freedom. There is no rent to pay. No bills for water, gas or electricity. Fuel can be picked up along the shore. Food can be hauled out of the river, or fish can be traded for groceries. Floating logs can be caught, sawn up, and sold as firewood.

Especially in flood-time the river is a generous provider. It brings barrels and boxes, tables, chairs and beds, rowboats, clothing, hats and shoes, chickens and pigs.

But the river is becoming less congenial to the shantyfolk. Straightening it has made the current swift and strong.

'I used to be able to paddle my canoe straight across the

river,' said Guy Jones at Terrene Landing. 'Not now – the current is too fast.'

We put in our own canoe and riskily proved him right. Whirlpools spun the boat like a top and without the help of a back eddy we could not have regained the landing.

Fishing is not what it was. With the speeding up of the current the fish don't have quiet spots to breed.

We visited the Joneses in their shantyboat. It was no longer a shanty nor a boat, for they had hauled it out of the river, placed it firmly on shore, and added to it to make a good home, large enough for sewing machine, console radio, TV, comfortable chairs and beds and a screened porch.

Even the shanty folk who still remain afloat have moved up in the world. The children go to school and later get jobs ashore in the rapidly expanding industries of the southland.

*   *   *

Southern hospitality overwhelmed us at Greenville. Mayor Archer personally took us about and dined us twice, and millionaire cotton-king William T. Wynn and his wife lodged us in their beautiful home overnight and staged a sparkling dinner party that brought out some good stories.

Hodding Carter, Pulitzer Prize-winning newspaper editor, author and correspondent for *Reader's Digest*, told one at the expense of that magazine. I do not think humour-loving DeWitt Wallace will be annoyed if I repeat it.

A contributor – so the tale runs – sent in a piece about a polar bear. The *Digest* editors replied that they needed something more intimate. So he revised it to 'Making Love to a Polar Bear'. They said, good, but it ought to be more personal. He made it 'How I Made Love to a Polar Bear'. They said, almost perfect, but please give the piece some spiritual significance. His final theme was 'How I Made Love to a Polar Bear and Found God'.

Greenville had grim and tragic experiences during the great flood of 1927. But Mr Wynn recalled one of the lighter incidents.

When the town was inundated, ten thousand Negroes were evacuated to temporary camps on the crest of the levee. They were divided according to precincts and each person had to go to the medical tent of his precinct to get typhoid shots. One woman who came to the wrong place was told,

'You don't belong here. You've got to get vaccinated in your precinct.'

'Lor' God,' she said, 'this is a funny country. You white folks get vaccinated in your arm and you tell us we got to get vaccinated in our precinct.'

That reminded someone of the unlucky man who couldn't collect a debt and went to a lawyer about it.

'Have you any money?' asked the lawyer.

'No.'

'Then I'd have to take your case on a contingent basis.'

'Well, I'll have to think about that.' He went to a trusted adviser.

'What does this mean – contingent basis?'

'Well, Joe, it means that if your lawyer loses your case he gets nothing. And if he wins the case, you get nothing.'

This being the state of Mississippi, the conversation strayed to Mississippi's famous author, William Faulkner. It seems that he was not universally idolized in his home state. One of our party, a young matron, had recently done an M.A. thesis on *The Decline of the Art of William Faulkner*. The professor in charge was shocked. This was an insult to literature and to the State of Mississippi. He insisted that she cut out all derogatory remarks about Faulkner. She would not do it. She went to the dean and was assigned another thesis master who allowed her to give full rein to her heretical views.

*   *   *

Returning to Memphis, we board the towboat *Wake Island* southbound.

There is a story behind every spot that we are to pass – stories that are suggested in their unusual names: Paddy's Hen, Robinson Crusoe Lower Light, Vice President Island, Cow Island Corner, Mark Twain, Jimmie Shivers, Kangaroo Point, Hop Joe, Caving Bank.

A blinding thunderstorm comes on. It is impossible to see even to the end of the barges. Our pilot talks over the radiophone with the captain of the towboat *Sam Houston*, on the way upstream, invisible, except on the radar screen.

'Skipper, how you situated down there now?'

'Not so good. Can't make the bend in this wind. Think I'll just lay by for a while. It can't stay this bad for long.'

'That's a good idea, captain. There're too many islands and sandbars here to take chances.'

Both tows stand by. The masters discuss, not the river, but their homes and families and what they planted in their vegetable gardens the last time they were on leave. Then our pilot,

'Well, I'm in a pretty bad place here by Cat Island. Apt to get pushed aground. I think I'll ease on down.'

'Okay. It's clearing a bit anyhow. Think I'd better stay right here till you pass.'

'Well, I'll be seeing you.'

They do see each other, or rather each other's boats, but only as indistinct blobs in the storm. But there's nothing indistinct about their conversation which roars on until they are miles apart.

The turmoil of the river is fantastic. Big logs swirl around, then stand up on end and are sucked down. A small boat would be safer in the mid-Atlantic than in this powerful current, checkmated by violent wind. We see a barge torn loose from its moorings and turned upside down. It is one of the big boys, three hundred feet long and forty-eight wide, and it is flipped over like a pancake.

We wait till the storm moderates before we pass under Greenville Bridge. This had been considered the most dangerous bridge on the river – an honour now transferred to the bridge at Vicksburg. A few years ago the tug *Natchez* struck a pier of the Greenville Bridge and sank with eleven men trapped. Divers later searched for it in vain.

Recently a tow of lead hit the same pier and a million dollars worth of lead went down. Since the cargo was so valuable every effort was made to locate it. No trace of it was found. Evidently the extremely heavy tow, each block of lead weighing a ton, sank into the soft bottom and was immediately buried in silt.

What makes the Vicksburg Bridge so dangerous is that there is a strong cross-current or 'set' from the right shore. All the officers are in the pilot-house to watch our captain take us through. He heads straight for a pier and apparent destruction. In the nick of time the set carries the enormous tow sliding to port just far enough to miss the pier and we pass through with plenty of room to spare.

This would not be too hard a trick for an easily manoeuvrable motorboat, but try it with 21,300 tons of tow stretching a quarter of a mile ahead of your steering levers!

* * *

The skill and responsibility of the Mississippi pilot make him cock of the walk among rivermen. It was so in steamboat days – it is so still. The only change is that there is less bluster and swagger than in the old days. Profanity used to be an art carefully cultivated by every pilot.

'What's the use of being a steamboat captain,' said one oldtimer, 'if you can't tell people to go to hell?'

The master's authority was supreme. In the days before

searchlights, the boat had to be darkened so that the pilot could see the river. On one occasion a State Governor was aboard and his stateroom light shone out through the curtain. So the pilot sent a boy down with his compliments, and would the Governor please put out the light. The Governor took offence and told the boy to go to a hot place.

The pilot, hearing the boy's report, turned the wheel over to his cub, went down to the Governor and said,

'Governor, either you put out that light or I'll put you off at the next landing.'

The Governor put out the light.

Pilots still say pretty much what they think, no matter where the chips may fall. Edna Ferber, doing research for *Show Boat*, boarded a river boat. The mate took her up to the pilot-house. Before he could introduce her to the captain she spotted a copy of her novel, *So Big*, and said,

'Captain, I see you're reading *So Big*. How do you like it?'

'If it don't get better,' was the gruff reply, 'I'm going to throw it in the river.'

Moral for authors: Don't ask.

*   *   *

The self-importance of a pilot is perhaps justified, for he has mastered a most difficult profession. He must not only know his craft – he must know his river. What a paragon a taxi-driver would be if he knew Broadway from the Battery to Spuyten Duyvil in detail, every business building and store and house, every window and lamp-post, every neon sign and fence and tree, and knew all of it so precisely that he could be set down on it anywhere in the darkest night and describe what was on either side of him. It is just so that a pilot has to carry the Mississippi River in his head.

Before he can get his pilot's licence the novice must be able to draw any section of the river showing its exact width, position of the best channel, location of shoals, bends, points, day-boards, lights and landings.

He needs to be an interpreter of signs and portents. A floating log shows that the river is rising, a slanting line on the surface means a reef beneath, 'boils' are a warning that a bar is dissolving and a new channel forming, a whirlpool may mean the deposit of a new shoal, an almost imperceptible V may be caused by a dangerous snag just below the surface.

He becomes a weather forecaster. A sticky pilotwheel in the evening means fog before morning. Three foggy mornings usually bring rain. If the gulls are restless a storm is likely within twenty-four hours. Thick frost on the trees portends a thaw and a flood. An east wind brings rain and a west wind, clear weather.

It would not seem necessary for a pilot to know anything about dogs. But pilots have frequently saved themselves and their craft when ploughing through dense fog, by their ability to distinguish between one dog's bark and another's and so determine their exact location.

True, the system does not always work. The dog may not be at home. The pilot, depending upon a certain dog to get him around a fogbound point one night, ran full into the rocks – because the dog had strayed from the farmhouse and the sound came from a new direction. And Ben Lucien Burman tells of a Captain Barney who, when he neared a certain dangerous shoal in a fog, would ring his bell and get an answering bark. Then he knew it was time to swing out. One night, believing he must be near the shoal, he rang but got no answer. After two minutes he rang again. He still did not hear the familiar bark. He knew the dog would not fail him and decided he must not be as near to the shoal as he had supposed. The next instant his boat was breaking up on the rocks. The dog had died the night before.

The best pilot is not infallible. When the water is high and the river spreads out on both sides, blotting out familiar landmarks, it is easy to lose one's bearings. During one flood, a pilot grounded his boat on a prairie many miles from the channel and the receding flood left him high and dry. He telegraphed to his employers,

'Am out on Lone Tree Prairie. What shall I do?'

They answered, 'Go farming, you landlubber.'

No pilot can know it all, though some pretend that they do. Modest Abe Lincoln, applying for a pilot's job, was asked,

'Are you acquainted with the river, and do you know where the snags are?'

'Well,' replied Abe hesitantly, 'I'm pretty well acquainted, but the snags, I don't know exactly so much about them.'

'Don't know about the snags?' exclaimed the captain, contemptuously. 'You'd make a pretty pilot!'

'What for do I want to know where the snags are?' drawled Abe. 'I know where they ain't, and that's where I do my sailing!'

He was hired and that captain later testified that Abe Lincoln was one of the best pilots on the river.

A good pilot becomes so familiar with certain sections of the river that his operations are automatic. One who happened to be a somnambulist wandered into the pilot-house one dark night and laid his hand on the wheel. The steersman, new on the job, and unaware of his senior's habit of sleep-walking, supposed that the veteran was relieving him because they were approaching a particularly dangerous channel through shoals. He went below. There he encountered the night watchman who stared at him and asked,

'Who's at the wheel?'

When told, he made a rush for the pilot-house, the cub following. No one was at the wheel. The boat was through the shoals and in safe water.

'If he can do that kind of piloting when he is sound asleep,' commented the amazed cub, 'what couldn't he do if he was dead!'

As a matter of fact, a dead pilot once saved a boat from destruction. Alone at night, guiding the boat through jagged reefs, he was suddenly seized with a stroke. With a desperate effort he threw himself on the whistle-treadle and as life passed from him his weight kept the whistle blowing till someone came to take the wheel.

Pilots are rough heroes, yet they can be surprisingly gentle. A pilot of a 2,800 horsepower towboat pushing a quarter of a mile of barges received a radiophone message from a captain downstream that a mama duck and her baby were around the bend. The youngster might be drowned by the backwash of the big boat. The pilot at once reversed his engines and cost his employers valuable time as he slowed down enough to give the ducks time to climb to safety on the bank.

* * *

We disembark at the hill city of Vicksburg, famous 'Gibraltar of the Confederacy', perhaps the hardest nut General Grant ever had to crack.

Vicksburg cherishes the memory of that gallant defence. Her extensive Military Park preserves the lines of the Battle of Vicksburg. The walls of the Vicksburg Hotel lobby are hung with pictures of war memorials.

The South has a long memory. In the Helena Hotel, Helena, Arkansas, we had seen a line of portraits referred to as those of 'seven generals that Helena gave to the War'. But this was not a reference to the last war nor the one before the last, nor the Spanish-American War. To the South 'the War' is still the War Between the States, as they prefer to call it, rather than the Civil War.

This is part of a larger phenomenon. The South has a personality and pride of its own. We had noticed a sign in the back window of a Ford made in Memphis: 'Built in the mid-South by Southerners'. The South is conscious of the South as the North is not conscious of the North. You would never see: 'Built in the mid-North by Northerners'. The North merely thinks of itself as part of the United States. The South thinks of itself as something a little apart from the rest of the United States. This local pride has both its merits and its dangers.

16

Old Al Abdicates

THE MOST STIRRING STORY to come out of the Mississippi Valley is the story of the conquest of the Father of
Waters by the U.S. Engineers.

Near Vicksburg, a gigantic model of the Mississippi
System laid out on a site of eight-hundred acres, with real
water running through its channels to simulate the rivers,
enables the Engineers to determine just what should be done
next and where.

In Vicksburg we met the monarch who had taken the
place of Old Al as the River King. He was Major-General
John R. Hardin, President of the Mississippi River Commission, about to retire with all the principal battles won. A
fine, studious man with a habit of precise speech and a kindly
wrinkling at the corners of the eyes, he believed the river was
now under such control that not only a flood like that of
1927 could be disposed of, but a possible super-flood 20
per cent greater.

This does not mean that the Mississippi will give no more
trouble. It does mean that the terrible disasters of the past are
not likely to be repeated.

The flood of 1927 drove 800,000 people from their homes.
Heavy rains pouring upon the Mississippi watershed which
stretches to within 250 miles of the Atlantic and 500 of the
Pacific, an area of about 1,224,000 square miles, drained into

the central river. It was estimated that a fabulous 250 cubic miles of water fell in the Mississippi area. Much soaked in, much evaporated, but 60 cubic miles of it were left to swell the big river.

Terrific currents chewed holes in the levees and poured through to inundate towns, carry away houses, and bury farms in muddy water as much as 18 feet deep. The river broadened in some places to a width of 80 miles. Many people were trapped and drowned. Animals fled to the high places – mounds, trees, chimneys. They forgot their animosities. Old enemies huddled together in terror, rabbits, muskrats, herons, chickens, possums, snakes, foxes, raccoons and deer. Horses swam away until they were exhausted or found refuge, but the cattle stood impassive in the water until they drowned or starved to death.

New Orleans saw the river rolling above her, topping the levees. Thousands of sandbags increased the height of the levees, but still the river rose. Was there no way to save the city with its half million population and its millions in wealth?

There was a way. Officials talked about it in whispers. But the word got out. The country-folk of the marshes and bayous below New Orleans were horrified. They were to be asked to accept ruin so that New Orleans might be saved. The idea was to make a deliberate break in the levee through which the river could pour out over the southern parishes and so relieve the threat to New Orleans.

The farmers, trappers, fishermen protested, appealed to the city fathers, sent urgent telegrams to Washington. Washington could see no alternative. Soldiers were sent to superintend the blasting of the levee at Caernarvon. Trucks came to haul away the household goods of the people who were about to lose their homes. Compensation would be paid to all evacuees. The wealthy merchants of New Orleans would take care of that. But what compensation could there be for such loss?

People and their possessions were loaded into trucks and

carried off. Many refused to go. They had faith that prayers and charms would avert flood. Some of the aged, too frail to travel, preferred to drown. The levee was dynamited, the angry Mississippi poured through the breach, and a shocked official of the low country said, 'You are witnessing the public execution of a parish.'

But New Orleans was saved.

Even when not infuriated by flood, Old Al could never be trusted. With a flick of his tail, which roustabouts who claim to have seen it declare is five miles long, he can wipe out an island, topple a bank, fling the main channel from one side of the river to the other, and make sport of boundaries.

When the river was adopted as the line between states, no one seems to have realized that the river would not stay put. It loops and unloops like a tortured snake. It used to be not at all uncommon for the river to make a great circle and come back to within a few hundred feet of itself. Then the current might cut through the narrow neck and a big circle of land belonging to Mississippi would find itself on the Arkansas side of the river. This sort of thing has happened dozens of times. Wrote Mark Twain,

'A man is living in the state of Mississippi today, a cutoff occurs tonight, and tomorrow the man finds himself and his land over on the other side of the river, within the boundaries and subject to the laws of the state of Louisiana! Such a thing, happening in the upper river in the old times, could have transferred a slave from Missouri to Illinois and made a free man of him.'

There is a little more humour than accuracy in this statement. The law draws a distinction between slow changes and quick ones. When the river changes its course gradually by eroding one bank and silting up the other, the boundary moves with the river. Thus a state may gradually lose land or acquire land, and the area of a state in square miles will not be the same from one year to the next. But if the river changes its course by what the law calls 'evulsion' – a sudden plucking out of an entirely new path for itself – the boundary remains where it was before.

The results are highly confusing. A man who had a farm in Mississippi now finds himself on the Louisiana side of the river, but he is still in Mississippi. From then on his loyalty is divided. He is still qualified to vote in Mississippi, but his new friends are Louisianans and he drives to a Louisiana town to do his shopping. At any time the stream may resume its old channel and he will be back on the other side of the river.

Greenville used to be on the river, which then took another course, leaving the town on the abandoned loop. Vicksburg, once on the river, is now on the Yazoo. The town of Delta which used to be three miles below Vicksburg found itself, after a cutoff, two miles above Vicksburg. Ste Genevieve, Arkansas City and Rosedale, once river towns, are now inland.

But that is better than nothing. Napoleon was completely swallowed. Boats now sail over it. Prentiss was buried in mud. Kaskaskia, 'an outpost of civilization and culture', was the first capital of Illinois and a very considerable city. House by house, street by street, it disappeared into the Mississippi.

So great have been the changes in the channel of the Mississippi that most of the thirteen hundred miles of river down which La Salle floated is now solid ground!

The contortions of the river lead to some quite incredible situations. Consider the story of a man after whom Lazy Man's Landing was named. When he wanted to go to town to get drunk he would float down the river 35 miles to Greenville. When again sober, he did *not* paddle 35 miles upstream to his home. He started off *downstream*, floated four miles with the current, pulled his canoe over a narrow neck of land, floated down another four miles, made another portage, floated down four miles, made a portage, floated down four miles, portaged again, then floated down a mile to his home. The sketch shows how it was done.

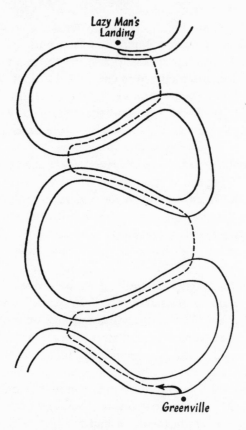

It could not be done today, for cutoffs have straightened this stretch of the river. These cutoffs were not left to the whims of Old Al, but were made deliberately by the Engineers.

The Corps of Engineers, U.S. Army, have transformed the river. They had made many cutoffs even before 1874 when Mark Twain wrote *Life on the Mississippi*, in which the humorist calculated that if they kept on shortening the river at the same rate 'any person can see that 742 years from now the Lower Mississippi will be only a mile and three quarters long, and Cairo and New Orleans will have joined their streets together, and be plodding comfortably along under a single mayor and a mutual board of aldermen'.

The river is not yet reduced to a mile and three quarters, but it is considerably shorter than when Mark Twain knew it. Until 1927 the Engineers had been seriously hampered by lack of funds. The disaster of that year stung Congress into the passage of the Flood Control Act of 1928 and the appropriation of enough money to implement it.

Between 1929 and 1942 the Engineers made sixteen cutoffs, shortening the river 151·8 miles.

The cutoffs have several merits. Less mileage between St Louis and New Orleans means quicker transport. Many hours, even days, are saved. The straightened river does not cut into its banks so severely as when it had to swing around curve after curve. Since the grade is steepened, the current is faster and stronger. This is bad for small boats, but flood control is not concerned with small boats. Diesel-powered towboats can easily plough their way upstream against the current and, when going down, they get through to their destination as much as 50 per cent faster than in the old days of slow water.

In times of flood the swollen waters are not blocked and turned aside in loop after loop, and thereby compelled to spread out over the country, swamping towns and farms. The straightened channel carries them swiftly through to the Gulf. A given volume of water can get through in far less time. Thus the runoff may be able to keep up with the rainfall.

But all these factors have to be calculated with great nicety. The cutoff is not a cure-all. On some loops a cutoff is not practicable. The great New Madrid Bend 26 miles around could be reduced to a thousand feet by a short-cut through the neck of the bend.

It has not been done and perhaps never will be. Since the water level is ten feet higher above the bend than below it, a cutoff would make a millrace. Also it would lower the level of the river above and vessels would hang up on the rocks at Thebes where there is already difficulty in maintaining enough depth for navigation.

17

The Great Wall

THE BUILDING OF THE GREAT WALL, twice the length of China's, also devolves upon the Engineers. The levees lining both sides of the river must be placed with great care. They do not, as one might imagine, sit on the bank of the river. They may be back as far as five miles from the stream. This is to give the River King room to thrust out his elbows at floodtime. The wide floodplain is an automatic relief valve. The water spreads gently over the lowlands and loses much of its force before it reaches the levees.

These great earthen battlements, a hundred feet thick at the base and three or four storeys high, look completely invulnerable. Yet so small a thing as a pocket gopher may destroy them. A gopher, rat or armadillo makes a small burrow, then perhaps an internal system of runways, side branches, chambers for storage and nests. Some day the water rises, enters the burrows, and gradually reduces the solid bank to a mound of mush. The slopes slough off and slide down. The seepage comes through to the inner side and there is no small boy handy to stop the drip of water with his thumb.

The drip becomes a dribble, the dribble becomes a continuous stream, the hole broadens with amazing speed and the stream is a torrent. The earth above the hole drops and is washed out, and the result is a crevasse through which a

Niagara pours into the back country sending people upstairs or into boats or to seek precarious refuge on the crest of the remaining levee.

Only eternal vigilance can prevent such catastrophes. The levees are usually kept clear of vegetation so that fiddler crabs and other borers can be more easily seen and destroyed. Burrows must be filled. During high water guards must walk the levee and watch for 'boils', small geysers marking the beginnings of breaks.

One of the greatest achievements of the Engineers has been the construction of the Bonnet Carré Spillway which in case of need will carry almost two million gallons per second out of the river and through Lake Pontchartrain to the sea, side-stepping New Orleans; and the even more ambitious Morganza Floodway which will divert flood waters from the Mississippi down the basin of the Atchafalaya to the Gulf.

In 1937 the work of the Engineers was put to the acid test. The largest flood of historical times poured down the Mississippi. The army was ready to evacuate a million people *if* the levees broke. Cairo, trapped between the Ohio and the Mississippi, pumped water out of town as fast as it flowed in over or through the levees. The river was three miles wide at Memphis and climbing into the town. The Bonnet Carré Spillway, completed only two years before, was opened, a gate at a time. Other spillways had not been finished, but they were not needed.

It was a near thing. In many places the water was levee-high. Hodding Carter looked from his newspaper office window in Greenville to see Coast Guard cutters moored twenty feet above street level. But the levees held and through the Bonnet Carré enough water was drawn off to cover 1,250,000 acres ten feet deep. This lowered the river level for more than a hundred miles and New Orleans was safe.

The Engineers were not satisfied. This had been the biggest of the big floods, but suppose there should be one bigger still?

Plans were made to cope with 'Project Superflood', should it ever come. The new spillways, the lakes of the Upper Mississippi converted into reservoirs, the dams and locks, the strengthened levees, are all insurance against the possible superflood.

In 1957, low delta country in Louisiana was flooded. But the culprit in this case was not the Mississippi, but tidal waves from the Gulf driven by a hurricane.

A constant preoccupation of the Engineers is the maintenance of a channel nine feet deep and three hundred feet wide all the way up to Minneapolis. This depth is soon to be increased to twelve feet. From Baton Rouge down, a channel at least thirty-five feet deep is maintained for ocean-going vessels.

We rode one of the patrol boats which constantly beat up and down the river sounding the depths to determine where dredging must be done. No deckhand stood out on the bow dropping a leadline. A machine at the captain's elbow gave him the necessary information. The fathometer sent down an impulse to the river bottom and the time it took to bounce back showed the depth. Not only showed it but wrote it down in a graph.

'That's our baby,' said the captain, caressing his Edo Depth Recorder.

Every modern towboat is also equipped with a fathometer in the pilot-house. This shows the depths beneath the towboat. But how about the depth a quarter of a mile ahead under the front barges? Automatic recording there also may be arranged but, when this is not done, the captain blows a sounding signal on his whistle, deckhands run out to the end of the tow, drop the lead in the old way, and sing back the results. It takes one back to the old days that gave Sam Clemens his pen name.

When Mark Twain, long famous, went back to the river with his family in 1886, his small daughter Clara heard the leadsman call, 'Mark twain, mark twain.' She ran to her father with the reproach,

'Papa, I have hunted all over the boat for you. Don't you know they are calling for you?'

'Mark twain' meant two fathoms or twelve feet. Some of the other calls were 'Quarter less twain,' 'Quarter twain,' 'Half twain,' 'Mark tyree,' 'Half tyree,' and 'Mark four.'

The leadsmen realized that their reports could make the man in the pilot-house much worried or much relieved, and they sometimes took advantage of the situation. A Negro leadsman said to the captain,

'I laks you better than I do the pilot. I always gives you mo watuh than I do him.'

The calls were not spoken, but sung, with a bit of a tune, different for each call, so that even if the master could not hear the words he might understand the call. The teletalk has changed all that. The leadsman speaks softly into the phone. A man five feet away may not hear him but his report comes out like the roar of a lion in the pilot-house. He may not use the old terms, perhaps does not even know them, but speaks prosaically in feet or fathoms. His services are not often needed; the masters have come to have confidence in the vigilance of the Engineers and their prowling patrol boats.

Where dredging is required, a 'dustpan dredge' with a sucking mouth thirty-five feet wide may be used if the bottom is soft. Where it is hard, a many-bladed 'cutterhead' is used to mince up the clay and gravel which is then sucked away by a gigantic vacuum-cleaner and passes through a tube a thousand feet or so to the shore. The dredge is like an over-sized elephant with a huge trunk stretching across the river.

The word 'dredge' may call up an image of something small, smelly and noisy, the sort so often seen hoisting mud into barges. The Mississippi dredge is a different breed. We spent a day on the dredge *Rock Island* which, according to the captain, cost $750,000 to build in 1936 and would cost

$3,000,000 to replace. It is the floating home of 52 men, also of 2 women who run the kitchen, is equipped with every civilized comfort, and is as spick-and-span as a millionaire's yacht.

No one can tell what next will pour out on shore from the end of the elephant's trunk – perhaps doubloons from the days of the conquering Spaniards; perhaps cannon balls of the Civil War; perhaps buffalo horns reminiscent of the herds that used to swim the Mississippi, delaying steamboats for hours; perhaps the skeletons of unfortunate rivermen.

18

Snagboat and Delta Queen

ANOTHER VESSEL UNIQUE to the Mississippi is the snagboat. Snags are among the chief perils of the big river. Undercut by the current, a bank will cave in, hurling big trees into the river. The roots of the tree will sink to the bottom because they are heavily embedded with dirt. The top of the tree, being lighter, will float on or near the surface and the current will point it downstream.

The snag that stays in a fixed position is called a 'planter'. One that keeps lowering and raising its head is a 'sawyer'. Either may stave in a boat coming upstream, but the sawyer is the more dangerous. Its rhythm may be very slow so that it is out of sight for many minutes at a time. The steersman looks out upon perfectly smooth water only to see a monster rear its head ten feet above the surface when it is too late to avoid it. '*Chicots*', the teeth of the river, the French used to call these snags, and they can bite a hole through the toughest hull. It is the business of the snagboats to pluck these obstructions out of the channel.

We rode the big sternwheeler snagboat *Charles H. West* from Vicksburg to Greenville. Though it was a steamboat, soon to be replaced by diesel, it provided good quarters for its men and the finest of food. Rivermen vie for jobs in the fleet of the Engineers, for there they are sure of good treatment. From a lofty A-frame on the bow of the vessel dangled a gigantic pair of tongs which could grip and haul out a log as easily as a dentist could pull a tooth.

We seemed to be making for a small stick projecting from the water. It was only as big as my arm and rose but a few feet above the surface. Surely this huge tooth-puller would not trouble to give its attention to such a trifle.

The *West* slowed up to the stick and the tongs descended and bit in. Up came the stick, foot by foot. It grew thicker and heavier and still it came, ten feet, twenty, thirty and still more until the top of it rose above the lofty pilot-house and the roots rested on the deck. It was a cottonwood log no less than one hundred feet long. The men cut it into short lengths with power saws and dumped the pieces overboard to float harmlessly away.

Another task of the snagboat is the placing of buoys. Can buoys, shaped like a can, mark one side of the channel and nun buoys, topped with a hood like a nun's, mark the other. They must be moved frequently in accordance with changes in the channel. A master with his eye on the fathometer must determine the proper location of every buoy.

One of the most extraordinary feats of the Engineers is the paving of the river-bed. The Lower Mississippi over much of its length is now a paved street. The paving usually does not floor the central channel but covers the bank where the current and wave action would otherwise wash it away. It may extend six hundred feet or more from each shore towards the middle of the stream.

This flooring used to consist of trees bound together with wire into mats sometimes a mile long. Today the mats consist of reticulated slabs of concrete. These blocks are linked together with stainless steel wire, the whole forming a flexible mattress. The alligator-god who rules the river will even chew up concrete in time, but such a mat will usually last twenty or thirty years.

*   *   *

The paved Mississippi is like a great avenue, the more so because it even has its street lights. Mark Twain's 'two-thousand-mile torch-light procession' consists of a line of light standards on either side of the river, each one a tripod-post about twelve feet high painted white and furnished with a ladder by which one may reach the lamp. Batteries are now taking the place of kerosene to light the lamps. Some of the lights are steady, some flash. The flashing lights are used particularly at bends and points, dubious twists of the channel, where it might otherwise be difficult for the pilot to know whether the light he sees is on the right or left side of the channel. The flashing light answers this question at once. If on the right bank, the light will flash once every two seconds. The left bank light flashes twice at the end of every four seconds.

Actually, the light does not go on and off – it burns continuously, but a revolving disc covers it at intervals.

A Coast Guard ranger comes by once a month in a fast motorboat to check the light. But it must also be watched day by day, for accidents will happen. So local lightkeepers are employed, each tending fifteen or twenty lights, and paid ten dollars a light per month.

This job is no sinecure. Even when storms come tearing along the river, whipping the waves up into combers, the lightkeeper must leave his warm cabin, get into his skiff, and make his rounds. In fact it is just at such times that his service is most important. A flood may be raging, snags, timbers and whole houses may be sweeping down the river, the rain may be so heavy that he cannot see the oars in his hands. One of the greatest perils occurs when the light is located on a high clay bank under which he must land and which may break up and thunder down upon him at any moment. Many keepers have lost their lives in this way.

Periodically a Coast Guard launch proceeds downriver from Cairo setting every light tripod two hundred and fifty feet back from the bank. At Baton Rouge it turns back up-river and finds that dozens of lights have disappeared completely and many others are on the edge about to slide into oblivion.

A typical lightkeeper was Fred Wild who, tending his many lights, rowed in his 54 years of service a distance more than seven times around the earth. At last his 'armstrong power', as rivermen call it, gave out and he used a small gasoline launch.

When a lightkeeper is killed someone else must take over at once. In one sector near Natchez the substitute was the dead lightkeeper's small flaxen-haired daughter, affectionately known as Towhead. Every day passing rivermen saw little Towhead going faithfully from light to light and feared for her safety since the river was in flood, banks and trees tumbling into the swirling water.

Then Towhead was no longer seen. Was she sick? A pilot tied his boat to the bank and went up to investigate. In Towhead's tumbledown cabin he found the preacher and the undertaker. Towhead had been trimming a light when the bank beneath her caved in and she was drowned.

*   *   *

Natchez is one of the 'musts' of any Mississippi journey. Nowhere on the continent is there a better preservation of the life and manners of ante-bellum days. In the era of the great cotton planters, this city claimed more millionaires than any other in the land except New York.

That was the golden age of Natchez. Plantation owners built stately mansions and filled them with furnishings from Europe. The glory faded after the war. Today the golden age has returned with the discovery of oil and gas and the coming of large industries. The splendid mansions have been restored and are occupied by descendants of the original owners. Many are open to visitors throughout the year and, during March, thirty of them are included in a tour organized by The Pilgrimage Garden Club and The Natchez Garden Club. Not the least attractive feature of this tour is the presence of scores of pretty girls in ante-bellum costumes.

We did not arrive during the tour, but Mrs Balfour Miller, founder of the annual pilgrimage, took us to many of the great homes and through the beautiful gardens enhanced by girls in costumes of the Old South.

These girls take to hoop skirts as easily as their contemporaries in other towns take to sweaters and slacks. They do it so much it becomes natural. Some strangers are surprised. Said one of the belles:

'We're surprised that they are surprised.'

The effect is utterly charming. Even an ugly duckling – if there were any in Natchez – could be transformed into a creature of ineffable charm by putting her in ante-bellum costume.

* * *

Natchez mansions scorn street numbers. Each must have a name, and the name breathes the magnolia perfume of the days of Southern aristocracy: Linden, Auburn, Elmscourt, Landsdowne, The Forest, Saragossa, Gloucester, Longwood, Stanton Hall, Arlington, Myrtle Grove, Cherry Grove, Elgin, Windy Hill Manor.

But there was another Natchez. It was called Natchez-under-the-Hill and lay under the cliff along the waterfront. It was the rendezvous of steamboat gamblers, thugs and prostitutes.

It was here that an angry captain hauled a gambling house into the river.

When the steamboat *Constellation*, under Captain John Russell, docked squarely in front of a notorious dive, some of the passengers went ashore to see the fun. Among them was a gentleman of the cloth. He did a turn at the gambling tables, explaining that his purpose was solely to gather material for a sermon on sin. Hirelings of the house did not hesitate to cheat the minister, and milked him of every cent he had been acquiring to build a new chapel.

Returning to the boat, the clergyman complained to Captain Russell. The captain stormed ashore, bearded the proprietor of the house and demanded that the money be returned.

'Now, I just cain't do that,' explained the proprietor. 'After all, it was a game of chance, and he took a chance like anybody else.'

'He took a chance with thieves,' retorted the captain. 'You didn't win his money. You stole it. You return that money or I'll dump your whole outfit in the river.'

'High and mighty, ain't you? That would be right interestin'. I'd like to see you try it.'

Captain Russell returned to his boat and sent ashore a gang of armed deckhands who passed a chain around the dive and snubbed it on to the capstan. The gamblers found these proceedings amusing. They still refused to return the money. They could not believe that the angry captain would actually carry out his threat.

They changed their tune when the captain rang the engines full speed astern and something like an earthquake shook the house, plaster fell, board walls cracked. The occupants spilled out on to the shore. The house slid down the bank and into the water until it was two-thirds submerged.

'Stop!' screamed the frantic owner. 'I'll pay.'

The minister got his money back and built his chapel. It is not recorded that he sought any more first-hand experience for his sermons on sin.

*   *   *

It was a few miles above Natchez that the *Drennan Whyte* sank in 1850 carrying with her a mixed cargo, the most important item of which was $100,000 in English gold.

The water was only forty feet deep and salvage seemed quite possible. The owners promptly sent the *Evermonde* to grapple for the sunken vessel. The *Evermonde* caught fire and went to the bottom with sixteen of her crew.

The next year a fully equipped salvage vessel, the *Ellen Adams* was sent to drag the river. In the meantime the current had shifted to the west and thick deposits of sand lay over the area where the wreck was supposed to lie. The river-bed was combed thoroughly, even as far as twenty miles up and down stream. Then the *Ellen Adams* struck a bar and sank.

More attempts were made the following spring, then the whole costly business was abandoned and marked down to profit and loss.

The eastern bend of the river silted up and became part of a farm. Years later the farm was bought by an Ancil Fortune from Ohio. He had a hard time making it pay.

In the spring of 1870, while digging a well, his spade struck metal. Uncovering it, he found it to be the smokestack of a steamboat. He had heard of the *Drennan Whyte* but could not believe that this was it, for it was far downstream from the spot where the treasure ship was supposed to have sunk. Yet it was just possible that a cache of $100,000 in gold might lie beneath his feet and the thought was exciting to a poor man.

He dared not call in others to help him. Nor could he dig alone, for the spot was exposed to full view. He was a methodical man and willing to wait. He filled up the hole, sowed willow seeds for five hundred feet in every direction, and waited five years.

Then, screened by the willows which grew ten feet high all about him, he started to dig. It was a long job, for he must carry on his farm work at the same time. It was three years

before he worked down the side of the boat to a brass plate
bearing the words *Drennan Whyte*.

With new ambition he tunnelled into the cabins of the
vessel. Storms filled the tunnels with sand and the pit with
water, which had to be baled out a bucketful at a time. In
May of 1891 he uncovered an iron chest, broke it open and
found it full of pieces of gold.

While deciding what to do about the money he went back to
his farm chores and in his excitement, broke his leg. He was
confined to his bed for a week. In the meantime the river,
swollen by heavy rains, flooded the land, switched the main
current from the west to the east side, cut away the willow
point until not a tree or bush remained, and probably – no
one knows for certain – pushed the wreck miles farther downstream. There it lies, but where? Skin-divers still hunt for it.

*   *   *

We now enter a land of mystery. This is part of the United
States, yet it has the exotic charm of a foreign country. A trip
to New Orleans is a trip abroad. Its French cuisine is equal to
anything that may be found in Paris. Among the bayous of
southern Louisiana near the mouth of the great river you
journey not only to France, but back in time to the France
of two centuries ago. The French spoken by the Acadians,
or 'Cajuns', is the old French of the seventeenth and eighteenth
centuries.

But you are visiting Spain as well as France. The mouth
of the Mississippi was the Spanish explorers' gate to the new
world. Alvarez de Pineda sailed up the river in 1519 and was
followed 23 years later by de Soto. In the wake of Spanish
explorers came settlers, and their descendants are still here.

But chiefly this is a trip to Africa. One might think oneself
in one of the better and more progressive of the new African
nations, such as Nigeria. Every second man in the state of

Mississippi is black, and the negro population is growing much more rapidly than the white. Only a third of Louisiana's population is negro, but it makes a two-thirds impact upon the visitor because of its distinctive character. For lack of education, it has not been perfectly assimilated. It represents a curious blend of African tradition with the heritage of the days of slavery.

It is largely a matter of terrain. If you look at a map of the mouthlands of the Mississippi, you see that they are half water. Where there are not rivers and lakes and bayous, there are swamps. Communities are isolated by water. The folk of one village may never have set foot in a village ten miles away because it is 'over the water'. The great marshes cannot be crossed even by boat.

These states are being rapidly industrialized and New Orleans is the second greatest port in the nation, barely outstripped by New York. But back among the waters practically the entire population makes a living from the soil or the sea.

Outside the great plantations, which are scientific enough, agriculture is carried on by a system of signs and portents. Leaf vegetables should be planted in the light of the moon, root vegetables during the dark phase. The holiness of Good Friday will bless the beans put into the ground during that day. Moonlight during the Christmas season means a light crop; darkness, a heavy crop. A south wind on 22 March brings a dry year. Thunder on a day in February means frost on the corresponding day in April. A red sunset brings wind. A rainbow has the same effect. A morning shower, like an old man's dance, never lasts long. Watch for the first song of the katydid, for three months later to the day there will be frost.

The talent of the water-world for preserving old traditions is nowhere more evident than in its plant-lore, long since forgotten in France, Spain and England, and on the way to oblivion even in Africa, but still alive in the Old South of the Mississippi bayous.

If the young lady of the house will plant blue vervain around the doorstep she will find that it will attract lovers. The young man who wants to gain control over a woman should chew devil's shoestring and rub it over his hands. Or a little red onion juice mixed with the tracks of a woman's left foot will lure the desired female. Loss of sexual virility can be corrected by chewing Sampson-snakeroot. It makes a man brave, proud and potent. If he will chew it while making a trade, he will get the best of the bargain.

The woman who does not wish to become pregnant drinks a mixture of red pepper and gunpowder.

Witchcraft is a constant worry in this strange world of space and silence under the long grey beards of Spanish moss hanging from the chins of oaks that leer down like gigantic goblins through the mist. But if a bit of high-John-the-conqueror (St John's wort) is held in the hand, witches will keep their distance. Placed under the bed, it will keep off ghosts, witches and nightmares.

The witch and the voodoo doctor are venerated and dreaded. Either may lay a curse upon one, and the power of suggestion is so great that the person cursed becomes ill and may die. Or his behaviour may be changed, for good or ill, by the spell cast over him. The process is closely related to brainwashing and hypnosis.

A victim of a bad habit may apply to the voodoo doctor for help in getting rid of it. Ben Lucien Burman, chief minstrel of the Mississippi after Mark Twain, tells in *Big River to Cross* how he himself became a temporary practitioner of voodoo. A roustabout named Turtle loved to play cards, but always lost. He wanted a spell cast over him to make him stop gambling.

Burman taught him a magical verse:

Gambler's money is not for me.
When I gamble my money rolls out to the sea.
Set my hand to shaking when I sit down to the cards.

Turtle was told by the amateur spellbinder that henceforth whenever he began to play his right hand would shake like a leaf.

Three months later the two met again. Turtle was very unhappy. He could no longer play cards; every time he tried, his hand shook as if it had the ague. He was taking money home to his wife. He begged Burman to remove the spell, but the voodoo doctor did not relent.

Turtle might have resorted to one of the many plants supposed to foil witches: a toadstool wet with camphor, or mustard seed planted about the house, or collard seed scattered under the bed, or prince's-feather in the breast pocket, or shame-weed (sensitive plant) to make the conjurer ashamed of his evil ways.

Other powerful plants are jimson weed which, pounded with the dried head of a snake, will bring blindness or death; Blood-o'-Jesus which brings peace; Bowels-of-Christ that can be stewed in lard to make a healing salve. A cedar tree planted in the yard will mean the death of someone you love. Sassafras burned in the fireplace will pop, and each pop spells the death of someone present. The leaves of the cottonwood tremble because Christ died on a cross of cottonwood. You may be struck dead for your sins if you pass a Judas (redbud) tree at night, for it was on this tree that Judas was hanged.

Trees that rub and creak in the wind are the homes of spirits. Dogs and cats can see spirits, and that is why they raise their voices in the night when no humans are about. Early morning mists over the river are the ghosts of persons drowned in the stream.

Ghosts take human form, say the river folk. A roustabout

met a beautiful Negress, fell in love, courted her for six nights. On the seventh she failed to appear. On a slip of paper she had given him her address. He tracked it down – and found himself in front of a small cemetery. Her name was on one of the tombstones. She had been dead for fifty years.

Fear of 'haunts' and hell fire takes many to church who otherwise would not darken its doors. One sinner, fearing that he was about to die, joined the Baptist, Methodist and Catholic churches to give himself three chances to get to Heaven.

The faith of the bayou people, white or black, is strong and simple. A revivalist, the Reverend Mr Dow, so thoroughly convinced his audience that the Day of Judgment was at hand that they actually heard Gabriel blowing his trump and the sinners flocked forward to the altar rail to obtain salvation before the crack of doom. Even those who learned later that the trump had actually been a tin horn, blown by a small boy whom the minister had posted in a treetop, respected the boy as a true agent of the Lord.

Religion here is not a cold, calculated thing, but something that requires clapping of hands, hymn-shouting, leaping and rolling. The preacher may begin to 'talk in tongues'. Like many of his parishioners, he may not be able to read or write. But they firmly believe that the strange sounds issuing from his mouth are the Hebrew of Moses or the Greek of St Paul, or even the Egyptian of the Pharaohs.

Death may be caused by the breaking of a taboo. A man may die because he brought an axe into the house and did not take it out through the same door. He may have cut too many windows in his house, thus admitting evil spirits. He may have antagonized a witch or voodoo doctor.

At the moment of death every mirror and picture in the room must be turned to the wall. Otherwise they will catch the spirit of the corpse which thereafter will haunt the house. If a horse neighs during the service in the cemetery, someone present will soon die. If anyone leaves before the grave is filled he is slated for an early death. He who points at the grave will suffer the loss of his finger by dry rot, or his mother's teeth will fall out.

Returning to the house after the funeral, one must completely empty the place of food and water, so the spirit of the dead will have no reason to hang about. Dishes used by the departed must be broken. Anyone who dares wear the dead man's clothes will feel the ghost of their owner tugging at him.

Schools are necessarily few in the water wastes. It is not only isolation that has a retarding influence, but language differences. Negroes may speak various dialects of English that would not be understood by a visitor from London or New York or even New Orleans. The many Dalmatians speak Croatian, those of Spanish descent prefer Spanish, and the Cajuns cling to a French unknown in France.

There are usages and nuances beyond the comprehension of an outsider. A visitor in the Pascagoula swamps was told that a certain man was being criticized by his neighbours because 'he planted his crop before he built his fence'.

The stranger, being a good-hearted man and a mite inclined to mix into other people's affairs with the very best of intentions, dropped in at the house of the man who had been criticized to see if he could patch things up.

'Now,' he said, 'I understand people are saying that you should have built a fence before you planted your crop. You know, you could still do that. It's a good thing to have a fence, then you know just where your line is, and your stock can't trample your neighbour's field and his can't get into yours.'

But the stranger's words did not seem to have the desired effect upon his listeners. The woman's eyes flashed with anger and she got up and left the room. The man crisply told the visitor to mind his own business and showed him the door.

The stranger went back to his friend and told him what had

happened. He wanted to know why the couple had become so angry over the mere question of building a fence.

His friend stared at him in open-mouthed wonder, then broke into a violent fit of laughter.

'My God, Jimmy,' he cried, 'don't you know that, in the Pascagoula swamps, planting a crop before building a fence means having a baby before you get married?'

Paradoxically, this land of some of the most simple and isolated people of America is also the home of the highly sophisticated. American culture is largely a product of the Deep South. We have already visited the mansions of aristocracy in Natchez. In the New Orleans area as well, great plantations and fine old homes are the setting for gracious living and an unusual level of learning. Deltan society seems to consist of a top and a bottom with nothing much in between. The advent of industry is gradually bringing a middle class into existence.

*   *   *

The stretch between Natchez and New Orleans we covered by car, by plane and by boat, and of these episodes the boat trip was the most interesting. The vessel this time was not a towboat, but the last of the steamboats to take overnight passengers. The *Delta Queen* still makes regular cruises from Cincinnati to New Orleans and from Cincinnati to St Paul. An old-fashioned 'stage' or gangplank on a grand scale hung in air beyond the bow. Behind, a great sternwheel threw up big waves and carried an aura of spray all about it like a veil. A rainbow appeared and disappeared in the vapour. We found the *Delta Queen* a floating hotel in the old tradition of deep comfort and fine food, but there was one agreeably modern feature, air-conditioning in the staterooms.

The view from the deck was pleasant, although unchanging. That is a characteristic of the Lower Mississippi. For twenty miles and more at a stretch you will see nothing but forest on both sides, not a house, not a human. It probably looks much as it did when La Salle first paddled south. Hidden by the trees a mile or several miles from the river is the levee, and'behind the levee, there is life aplenty. But the great flood plain is a place of solitude, birds and peace.

At Baton Rouge, however, the scene changes. Here the city crowds in upon the river and from Baton Rouge to New Orleans great industries are developing which will make this stretch another Ruhr Valley.

Some of the oldtime steamboats have been taken over by the U.S. Corps of Engineers who use them as inspection boats, prowling the river looking for trouble, and usually finding it.

From the lofty A-frame on the bow of the snagboat a gigantic pair of tongs descends to haul dangerous logs up out of the river. This one was a huge cottonwood a hundred feet long. Having drawn it up on deck, the men sawed it into short lengths which were thrown overboard to float harmlessly away.

Much of the Mississippi riverbed is paved! Mountains of gravel are converted into concrete slabs which are wired together in a vast flexible mattress which when laid on the river bottom and bank will prevent erosion for twenty years or more.

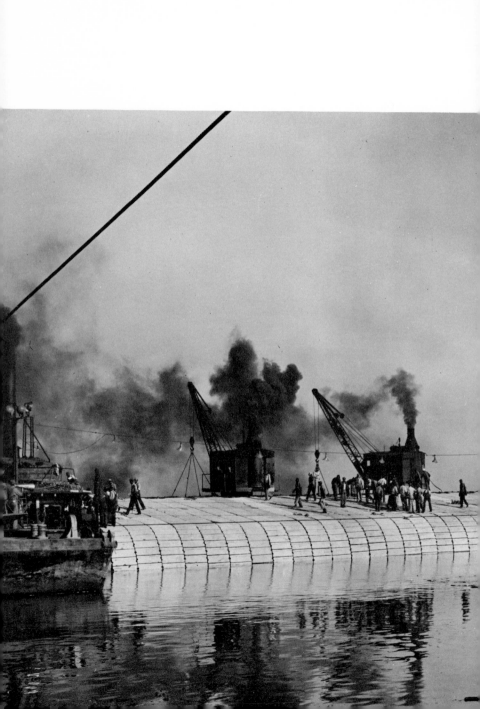

The river was forever changing its mind, abandoning old channels, making new ones, looping and unlooping like a tortured snake. Now the articulated concrete flooring on the riverbed and a great wall, twice the length of China's, help keep the wild stream within bounds.

The leadsman sings out the depths in traditional fashion, although on most boats he is now replaced by the fathometer. Mark Twain took his name from the call, "Mark twain," meaning two fathoms.

→

A twelve-foot hand points to Heaven in Port Gibson, Mississippi. This was unique in the world until a church in Switzerland copied the idea.

Two-headed monster, the paddlewheel ferry *Pelican* transports freight trains back and forth across the Mississippi at Helena, Arkansas. Only some two dozen paddlewheelers still remain on the Mississippi.

A hand-painted mural in the coffee shop of the Vicksburg Hotel does not exaggerate the charm of the old mansions that still grace the southland of the Mississippi.

Pilottown is an amphibious settlement perched on stilts over the water wastes near the mouth of the Mississippi. Here every incoming ship must take on a river pilot, every outgoing ship, a bar pilot.

Last of the oldstyle steamboats to take overnight passengers is the *Delta Queen*. Others make day excursions, but the *Delta Queen* is a floating hotel on cruises covering as much as two weeks. A huge steam-driven sternwheel propels her, an old-fashioned "stage" (gangplank) can be lowered to any shore, inner appointments are quaint and luxurious. There is one quite acceptable new feature, air conditioning.

The board shows whose turn is next. The pilot associations are aristocracies and admission is difficult. The best way to become a pilot is to be the son of one.

The nutria, like the water hyacinth, was a dubious gift from Brazil. Ten came. Now there are millions. They destroy other wildlife. But their fur makes a wonderful coat.

Tony Marinkovich and other immigrants from the Dalmatian Coast are quite at home in the lonely water world of the delta. They cultivate the world's finest oysters, trap nutria and muskrats, wrestle alligators out of the water by hand.

19

New Orleans and Beyond

WE PASS UNDER the new Mississippi River Bridge, the third largest of its kind in the world, flinging into the air an unsupported span of 1,450 feet between piers. There are boats all around us now, and ocean-going ships as well. New Orleans, in sixteenth place after the first World War, has moved to second place in dollar value of foreign trade, handling $1,500 million worth of import-export cargo annually.

The city as gateway for the mid-continent taps half the total area of the United States. Down more than 15,000 miles of inland waterways from thirty-one states come some 5,000 boats with cargo to be trans-shipped to 4,000 seagoing vessels and carried to ports all over the world.

One of the great forces behind this miracle has been International House. It is New Orleans' unique global marketplace. In its Trade Mart, businessmen from many countries meet to buy and sell.

But the tremendous activity of the old-new port does not invade the precincts of the Vieux Carré where iron lacework balconies look down on Spanish and French courtyards. Here tradition-loving restaurants serve some of the most delicious food in America.

*　　*　　*

New Orleans is vaguely supposed to be at the end of the Mississippi. But there are 110 miles of river below it and this is one of the most fascinating stretches of the entire river. Here the Mississippi has laid down its modern delta – modern in comparison with the alluvial plain it has deposited over the ages from Cairo south.

The deep delta country is a strange and fabulous region, the like of which cannot be found in many places on this planet. It is a bewildering mosaic of twisting channels, lakes, bayous (from the Choctaw *bayuk* meaning a small sluggish waterway), swamps and sloughs, rising to dry land near the river and culminating in the levee hugging the shore. The levee is the highest land anywhere, yet it is seldom twenty feet above the water. The river is broad and tranquil in its old age, but still has enough force to carry its tremendous burden of silt on towards the Gulf.

Visitors to New Orleans may sample part of the deltan river on the excursion boat *President* or the city's yacht, *Good Neighbor*. It is possible to drive eighty miles south along the river bank to Venice, which has none of the glory of its prototype but probably outdoes it in wetness. Here the road stops. The stream still has 30 miles to go, but travel beyond this point must be done by boat or plane or marsh buggy – the amphibious monster with such bloated balloon tyres that it can run over soft mud and even open water.

The dry ground along each side of the river is at first some miles wide before it gives way to marsh. It becomes more and more narrow to the south and finally tapers to a point at the Gulf. The people who live on it behind the levee also build themselves a rear levee to keep out the storm-driven tidal waves surging up through the marshes. When these barriers are overswept, or heavy rains flood the land between the levees, large pumps work day and night to send the water back into the marsh.

But people do not live merely on these slivers of land. The

marshes are full of islands and every fairly solid island bears houses or even villages, perched on posts. There is nothing entirely solid in this world. This is 'trembling earth'. Here geology can be seen at work. Nature has not yet quite decided what to do with all the mud poured out by the great river.

The land suddenly sinks beneath the feet, or suddenly swells up into a small hill. Land under water may rise to a height of nine feet or more above it. These 'mud lumps', as the deltans call them, have not been completely explained. They may be caused by gas and oil bubbling up from deep deposits. They are quite possibly due to the heavy weight of silt delivered by the river which by bearing down upon the soft clays in one area causes a push-up in another.

The folk who make this strange region their home were described by a visitor a century ago as 'aquatic men, with fins like fishes', noses like alligators', feet like ducks''. We did not see any who answered to this description, but certainly it does take a peculiar talent to make a life and a living in such surroundings. Lafitte and his fellows did well as pirates and smugglers. Even today a manhunt through these marshes is considered practically impossible. Forbidden cargoes still find their way through the delta.

There are many reminders of the great days of piracy. We launched our canoe on Barataria Bayou and noted that the bayou, the larger bay, the town, the lighthouse, and the pass, all bear the name 'Barataria' because of their association with the smugglers and pirates who made this locale their headquarters. 'Barataria' is an old Romance word meaning 'deception'. It is romantically reminiscent in some connections but seems a bit odd when used on a church which announces itself as Barataria Baptist Church.

Another sign, 'Lafitte Elementary School', seems to accord more honour to a robber and killer than one would expect an institution of learning to pay. More harmless and amusing is a sign over a tailor shop: 'Pants pressed while you hide'.

We paddled up a twisting offshoot of Barataria Bayou so narrow that the trees sometimes met overhead. Ghostly curtains of Spanish moss waved in the wind. That beautiful pest, the water hyacinth, bordered the banks with purple bloom.

It was an ideal home for big snakes. A five-foot cottonmouth crossed our bow in one direction at the same instant that an unknown serpent just as large came straight for the boat from the opposite shore with the apparent notion that it was a log on which he could crawl out and bask in the sun. A paddle fended him off.

A fisherman strung his net from shore to shore completely blocking the waterway and soon there was a tremendous splashing – the man paddled his pirogue to the spot and hauled out a four-foot gar.

We became temporarily lost in the labyrinth of channels. Now it was easy to understand why the pirates had chosen this water-maze as their retreat.

They had first made their nests in the bays of the Caribbean islands. But there they were never safe from attack. Moreover, it was a long way to market. New Orleans was the best place to sell their ill-gotten spoils. By holing up in the delta they were in close contact with the merchants of New Orleans who did not hesitate to deal in stolen goods, comforting themselves with the fiction that they were not really stolen but captured from enemy ships.

French New Orleans regarded anything Spanish as fair game and even issued 'letters of marque' to sea rovers, authorizing them to pounce upon any Spanish galleon. Thus the marauders were privateers, not pirates. But the line between the two was very thin and the lust for spoils led many a 'privateer' to prey not only upon Spanish shipping, but also English, American and even French.

It was convenient to have a few agents through whom booty might be sold to New Orleans traders. One of these agents was a blacksmith named Jean Lafitte – his smithy may still be seen in the Vieux Carré. He was a very unusual blacksmith. He had the strength required by his vocation, but otherwise he was an exquisite dandy, polite and polished, with a winning manner and generous disposition. He stood six feet two inches in height and his waving black hair, flourishing moustache and large hazel eyes made him a commanding figure who needed only fine clothes to make him at home in any drawing-room. He spoke Spanish, Italian, French and English with equal ease.

He got the fine clothes when, because of his outstanding success as agent for the smugglers, he was made commander of their bayou settlement. Moving to the bayou, he built a fine house, and adorned his person in keeping with his exalted station. At this stage of his career he is described as wearing a huge diamond brooch on his chest, large rings on his fingers, gaudy bangles on his ear lobes, a profusion of decorative chains on his jacket and a set of bowie knives and pistols holstered to his belt.

The pirate nest under his command became a town of a thousand freebooters and three hundred women of easy virtue. Besides thatched cottages, it was fully equipped with gambling houses, assignation dives and a large slave barracoon – for the corsairs dealt in slaves as well as inanimate merchandise. At regular intervals they transported their captives to New Orleans, boldly set up their market in a city square and sold as many as four hundred in a single auction.

But more difficult days were ahead. As Americans gradually took over control of New Orleans from the French, piracy was viewed with less tolerance. Governor Claiborne set a price of $500 on Jean Lafitte's head. Announcements bearing this offer were posted throughout New Orleans.

They did not stay up long. One night they disappeared and were replaced by posters signed by Jean Lafitte offering $1,500 for the head of Claiborne. The governor did not appreciate the joke and set out in earnest to bring the defiant corsair to justice.

He was interrupted by matters of a more serious nature. The English were preparing to attack New Orleans. An English naval commander, in a secret meeting with Lafitte, offered the pirate 30,000 pounds in gold and a commission in the Royal Navy if he and his gang would join forces with the invaders.

Lafitte asked for time to think it over. He used the time to notify Governor Claiborne of the intended attack. Doubtless he was prompted by cupidity rather than patriotism. Perhaps the Americans would give him a better offer. He proposed to the governor that he and his men would join the American forces on condition that they be pardoned for all former offences.

The proposition was reluctantly accepted, the pirates joined the troops of General Andy Jackson and the Battle of New Orleans ended British ambitions in the delta. The smugglers had fought most valiantly and a pardon for all their past misdeeds was signed by President Madison in 1815.

The bad little boys did not automatically become good little boys. They promptly returned to their old pursuits. The disillusioned authorities organized an expedition against them, captured their settlement, seized their booty, and committed many of them to the New Orleans calaboose.

Lafitte slipped through their fingers. He moved to Galveston Bay, built a small town, organized a new gang and made depredations on American vessels. In 1820 an American naval force sailed into the bay, bent on his capture. Warned of its approach, Lafitte set fire to his town and disappeared.

What happened to him thereafter is anyone's guess. According to one report, he died in 1826 on the island of Mujeres off the coast of Yucatan.

* * *

But the bayou country treasures the memory of another character quite different from the swashbuckler-smuggler-freebooter-dandy, Lafitte.

The gentle Evangeline of Longfellow's poem is still vividly remembered by the 'Cajuns'. The Acadians, people of French descent had been deported from Acadia, later called Nova Scotia, because of the suspicion that they secretly sided with the French in the French-English wars of the eighteenth century.

The poet's version was founded upon the true story of Emmeline Labiche. When, in 1755, the Acadian settlements were destroyed and six thousand Acadians were scattered far and wide, Emmeline was separated from her betrothed, the young farmer Louis Arceneaux (the Gabriel of the poem).

For years she searched for him. Landing at last on the shore of Bayou Teche in Louisiana, she saw her lover. They are supposed to have met beneath the branches of a great oak tree. It is still there and is known as the Evangeline Oak. But the faithful Emmeline found that her former sweetheart was now betrothed to another. Under the shock she lost her reason and died shortly afterwards. She was buried in the cemetery at St Martinville and her grave can still be seen. There too is the Evangeline Monument, set up by Dolores del Rio who played the role of Evangeline in the motion picture of that name.

The two stories, the true one and the poetic version, are further immortalized by the Longfellow-Evangeline Memorial Park established as a State Park in 1934. Not quite so romantic is the adoption of the heroine's name by filling stations and such commercial enterprises as 'Bulliard's Evangeline Pepper and Food Products Company, Visitors Admitted'.

*   *   *

This ghostly land of winding waters and writhing mists,

where aged trees

'Bearded with moss, and in garments green, indistinct in
the twilight,
Stand like Druids of eld, with voices sad and prophetic,
Stand like harpers hoar, with beards that rest on their
bosoms'

deserves this description far better than does the 'primeval
forest' of Acadia which Longfellow had in mind when he
wrote these lines.

That extraordinary epiphyte, Spanish moss, came by its
name in an odd way. The Spaniards, who had no use for the
French scornfully called the plant Frenchman's Beard. The
French in retaliation called it Spaniard's Beard. The French
outstayed the Spanish, so their name survived, modified
in time to 'Spanish moss'. The plant is unknown in Spain.

The botanical name was also a misnomer. Linnaeus, the
great plant namer, can be excused, for he had to think up
names for some hundred thousand plants. His reason for
calling this one *tillandsia* bordered on the fantastic. A fellow-
professor, Elias Tillands, was so deathly seasick on his voyage
from Stockholm to Åbo that he refused to board the ship for
the return journey and walked home a thousand miles around
the head of the Gulf of Bothnia. Linnaeus was aware that
Spanish moss was an air plant, not a parasite, and drew no
moisture whatever from the tree on which it was draped.
It has even been known to grow on telegraph wires. He
assumed it hated water, and named it after the great water-
hater, Professor Tillands.

It was later proved that Spanish moss, far from hating water,
grows best near water and absorbs moisture from the air.
What look like millions of small scaly hairs are actually
tiny mouths designed to drink the moisture of the bayou mists.

You look in vain for the roots of this strange plant. It has
no use for Mother Earth. Like a witch riding a broomstick,

it flies on the wind to lodge in the clefts of live oaks, willow oaks, water elms or cypresses, dead or alive, and there its seeds begin life quite independent of the soil beneath. No wonder the plant looks as if it did not belong in nature's scheme of things. Most of the year it is an unearthly grey, 'a witch's dream of ghostliness and horror', rendezvous of death-loving black vultures.

But in April it comes briefly alive. It reluctantly turns from grey to a pale green and puts out tiny yellow flowers that develop into pineapples – or something remotely related to that fruit, for Spanish moss is a member of the pineapple family. But I am sure that any husky, hearty Hawaiian pineapple would disdainfully deny the relationship.

Spanish moss is not only grimly ornamental; it is useful, and every year large quantities are harvested. The delta has its moss pickers and even its moss kings who own fleets of moss trucks and moss boats. The pickers must be agile tree climbers. During the season they earn as much as $75 a month. The moss, after being transported by truck or boat to headquarters, must be cured, ginned to clean out all twigs and foreign matter, then baled for shipment. Most of it goes to factories in the East where it is used to stuff mattresses and upholstery.

The moss-draped oaks look ancient enough but they are antedated by the cypresses. These stately trees are cousins of the giants of California, the sequoias and redwoods. Many of the cypresses of the Mississippi Valley are more than a thousand years old, which makes them the oldest living creatures to look down upon the great river. We who do not live in cypress country may think of this tree as an evergreen, but its needles turn yellow in autumn and fall away, leaving the tree naked throughout the winter.

The sycamores that make such a striking decorative motif along the Lower Mississippi cast their old hide every year as a snake sheds its skin and the fresh bark beneath is as soft as kid leather. It is a mottled light green, whitening as it bleaches under the sun, finally browning in late spring as the tree prepares to discard its old coat for a new one.

Giving an oriental touch to quiet backwaters and bayous is the lotus, sending its stem down six feet or more to the bottom. If one gets up early enough, he may see the lotus buds quiver as if shaken by an earthquake and then explode into glorious flowers a foot in diameter and as fragrant as incense.

The most common flower of many bayous is the beautiful and devilish water hyacinth. Eighty years ago there was not a single water hyacinth reported in the United States. Now many waterways once clear are made completely impassable by close serried ranks of this vigorous plant. And millions of dollars are being spent, largely in vain, to eradicate it.

During a New Orleans exposition in 1884 Brazil brought in a horticultural exhibit which included a dozen water hyacinths. The lovely tropical plants with their lavender flowers were greatly admired and at the close of the show they were eagerly appropriated by flower-lovers who planted them in water gardens. In an amazingly short time they escaped from the gardens and spread up and down streams and bayous. Boats could not plough through them. Louisiana appealed to the Corps of Engineers to do something.

The Engineers have been doing something faithfully ever since, but at present the hyacinths are away ahead of them. Guinea pigs are sexually frigid in comparison with water hyacinths. In eight months twenty plants can propagate 1,310,720.

These demoniacal breeders have turned hundreds of square miles of navigable waterways into hyacinth swamps where the water is so densely roofed over that fish and muskrats cannot live, ducks and geese cannot feed, and boats of several hundred horsepower stick fast until the Coast Guard comes to their rescue.

Surely the men who have all but mastered the tremendous forces of a mighty river would not be daunted by mere flowers.

It seemed a small matter to the Corps of Engineers. They sent out gangs of men with pitchforks, and the hyacinths were merely tossed ashore to rot. But the few that were overlooked multiplied into masses as heavy as before.

Then the inventive Engineers devised a hyacinth boat which scooped up the plants and ran them through crushers. This was just what the hyacinths wanted. Each particle promptly grew into a new hyacinth.

Dynamite was tried. It scattered the pest to populate new areas. Flame throwers made the glossy green leaves wilt and curl, but they soon revived. Arsenic was used. The plant seemed to develop a taste for it, ate it up and asked for more.

The baffled Engineers went back to the crusher idea, and built a sort of sea-going lawn-mower with jaws forty feet wide that minced the plants into such small particles that few of them could survive. This has been temporarily effective wherever used. There are not enough such machines and enough men to run them to be everywhere at the same time and our canoe frequently became so snarled in hyacinths that it was necessary to knife out the plants one by one to attain the breath-taking speed of a hundred feet an hour. Brazil's charming and well-meant gift is estimated to cost Louisiana alone some $70 million a year in loss of shipping channels and damage to fisheries.

The muskrat will not live beneath a hyacinth mat, and muskrats are big business in the delta. Some six million furs are marketed every year, three times as many as the total from all the rest of the United States with Canada thrown in. Louisiana also has the distinction of being America's greatest frog-catching state and the delta bullfrog attains the size of a football.

This always has been a land of giants. Here in ancient days he mastodon, elephant and giant sloth roamed, the beaver was seven feet tall sitting down, the bison supported heavy horns with a span of six feet, dragonflies were twenty-nine inches wide and cockroaches a foot long.

The monsters have not all disappeared. The alligator snapping turtle, largest fresh-water turtle in America, weighs two hundred pounds. Like overweight humans, this creature does not care for exercise. It lies on the bottom, opens its mouth in a wide yawn and wriggles a pink tonsil. A fish swims in to investigate the gaudy fluttering object and the turtle exerts itself sufficiently to close its jaws and swallow. Its smaller cousin, the snapping turtle, has a taste for hands dangling in the water over the gunwale of a boat and can neatly snip them off at the wrist.

The sturgeon, which was once a proud thirty-two feet long, still measures eight feet. The paddlefish, sometimes called the spoonbill catfish, is also a living fossil whose only surviving relative is found in the Yangtze. It is as long as a tall man is tall.

Strong-jawed eels four feet in length were never seen in a juvenile state and according to local superstition they began as horsehairs soaked in water. Finally it was discovered that they have the same habit as that of the wealthy planters – they go away for the summer. Voyaging 2,500 miles to the Sargasso Sea, they give birth to a new generation which, after attaining nearly full size, make the long trip back with unerring accuracy to the Mississippi bayous.

During the quiet hours of dawn or of dusk one may be startled to hear a strange drumming sound in the marshes. Indians believed that the river was talking. Delta fishermen are aware now that the sound is made by the drum, or sheep's head, using its large air bladder as a percussion instrument. This enormous fish thinks nothing of grinding clams, shells and all, into mush between its millstone teeth.

An odd fish of the swamps is the grindle, with a family history dating back to the age of the dinosaur and the ability to breathe air and live in mud. A dried-up marsh does not worry the grindle. It merely digs its way into the ground and waits, months if necessary, for the rains.

Delta fishermen are at home among the monsters. They even brave the fifteen-foot alligator gar, half reptile, covered with a coat almost as hard as bone. About one-fourth of the length of this monster is jaw. Yet some ardent sportsmen go after it with only a bow and arrow. The arrow is pointed with a deadly iron spear, eight inches long. The gar is the most ferocious and formidable of all Mississippi fish and does not hesitate to attack any other living thing, including man. Many deaths ascribed to the alligator should really be credited to the gar, as indicated by the fact that human remains have frequently been found in the stomach of this shark-size terror.

Real alligators are wrestled out of the water by hand, or caught in traps. They must be kept in check, for they prey upon hogs and poultry. They are almost invulnerable to bullets, except just in front of the forelegs. The hunter can lure them within range with a call like a dog's yelp or a pig's squeal. This method, by the way, was used in ancient Egypt. If the swamp dries in summer the alligator burrows into the mud and lies torpid until the water returns.

We witnessed the skinning of a sixteen-foot alligator, a job to be done with care since the hide is valuable and can be tanned into excellent and expensive leather. The teeth can be carved into ornaments. The flesh and eggs can be eaten, if you have an insensitive palate and a strong stomach, or the eggs can be hatched and the young alligators sold as pets. Some deltans claim that the tail of an alligator is a morsel for the gods, but if it is to be really flavoursome it should be buried in the ground for a few days until it 'ripens'.

Shrimping is big business in the delta. But the shrimpers would not think of beginning the season without the solemn ceremony of the Blessing of the Shrimp Fleet by the Archbishop.

We went by launch through the mazes of Barataria Bay to visit the oyster gatherers. We expected their island homes to be shanties and cabins. Instead we were ushered into a large white frame-house with three bedrooms, two modern bathrooms, and well-equipped kitchen. It was the home of Kuzma Tesvich who came from Dalmatia in 1929 with nothing; he now owns this house, three houses in Port Sulphur and one in New Orleans. We were served the famous Dalmatian drink, raisin wine.

There is money in oysters and the Dalmatian oystermen have found it. But there is trouble too and need for great skill and patience, as we learned when we went out on the oyster luggers and saw the complicated processes that must be gone through to produce what many gourmets call the world's finest oysters.

But the biggest fishing operation of the delta is for a fish most people have never heard of. And yet we come in contact with it, or products made from it, every day. It is the menhaden, a kind of herring.

Many soaps contain menhaden oil, as do linoleum, paint, varnish. The chicken, beef and pork that we eat were probably raised on feeds containing menhaden meal. The remarkable liquid plant-foods that make flowers grow like magic generally contain menhaden solubles.

Menhaden is the nation's largest commercial fishery. More of these twelve-inch, one-pound herring are taken from American waters than any other fish, twice the poundage of salmon, which holds second place.

Schools of the fish are located by low-flying planes. I took off with the pilot in 'Wild Bill', a Piper Super Cub named after the superintendent of the Empire Menhaden plant. It was a one-seat plane and the pilot was in the one seat. I sat behind him on a narrow shelf.

A Cub is almost no plane at all. You feel as if you were merely sitting on a stool in the sky. The roof is glass, the walls are glass, and since the whole plane is just wide enough for your body you look down on both sides into space.

We flew east over the marshes to open water. The pilot called my attention to a shadow in the sea. It was a school of menhaden. About a mile away was a ship attended by two smaller vessels called 'purse boats'. The pilot reported to the captain of the ship by radio. Almost immediately we saw the two purse boats turn and come in our direction.

We kept circling above the school. The purse boats carry no radio. When they came close the pilot reached them through his PA system with a loud speaker that can be heard from five hundred to a thousand feet. He guided them in to the school. He told them when to let down their net.

The net is a monster 1,200 feet long and 60 wide. One end was held by each boat and the great net was neatly wrapped around the school. The haul was then transferred to the mother ship.

All day the little planes hover over the sea, spotting schools for the purse boats. The largest catch ever made by this company in one day was 4,200,000 fish. Back at the plant we saw how the oil is expressed while the 1,200-foot nets are wound on reels as high as a three-storey house to dry.

Another profitable enterprise of the delta is the trapping of coypu, the fur of which is called 'nutria'.

The coypu might be called an outsized rat. It is one of the largest rodents on earth, frequently weighing forty pounds. Here again we have to give dubious thanks to Brazil. An Amazon animal-collector gave an animal-fancier from Louisiana ten coypu which the latter brought home and raised for their fur.

One night they escaped from the pen and it was the story of the water hyacinth all over again. There are now millions of them in the delta and strong measures have had to be adopted to delay their further multiplication. They will destroy any other form of wildlife that is not more than twice their own size. They spell death for chickens, small pigs or household pets.

They can live on land or in the water with equal ease and are equipped with webbed feet. The female has her nipples high on her flanks so that her young may lie on her back and feed while she swims about. These omnivorous creatures have all but taken over certain parts of the delta. Standing on a knob in a marsh we could count no fewer than forty-seven coypu within a radius of two hundred feet.

And yet the nutria (the marsh people call it by the name of its fur) is a blessing, or may be if its numbers can be controlled. The fur that covers its belly is as fine as silk. Some discriminating fur-buyers consider it superior to much better known and more expensive skins. It can be dyed any colour and its softness and charm are incredible.

The story is told of a fashionable lady who entered a New Orleans fur-store, took off her mink coat, and tried on a nutria. She said to her husband:

'Why did you get me that thing [the mink coat] when you could have gotten me this?'

'That thing' probably cost $3,500 or $4,000 while a nutria coat may be had for $200.

* * *

At Port Sulphur is the world's largest sulphur-mine. The sulphur lies so far underground that only a miracle would bring it to the surface. The miracle was performed. An inventor as imaginative as Jules Verne devised a way of piping down hot water into the sulphur beds; the hot water melted the sulphur and the sulphur soup was blown to the surface by compressed air.

From a plane belonging to the sulphur company we looked down upon yellow acres of sulphur, some of it in the form of solid mountains, some in lakes kept molten by heat and drained off into 'thermo barges' which, keeping it still hot, carry it up the Mississippi and throughout the mid-continent. Sulphur, of course, has thousands of uses. As sulphuric acid it enters into many products.

20

Deep Delta

THE REALLY COLOSSAL WEALTH of the delta is in its oil and gas. We flew over the oil rigs that stand in the marshes and in the Gulf itself as far as thirty miles from shore. All personnel are carried to and from the rigs by helicopter. On our plane radio, like that of a taxi, we overheard constant instructions to the drivers of these air taxis.

Weather is a serious subject to the oil-rig men since they are in a very exposed position. When a hurricane is forecast all are removed from the rigs. Even an ordinary storm may be fatal. We passed over a rig that had been upset a few days previously. It had completely turned turtle and nine men had died, trapped beneath it. Our pilot said,

'The deepest oil well in the world is here at Grand Ecaille – 22,000 feet. There are many ten thousand to fifteen thousand feet deep. These rigs cost money. One just finished cost $3,250,000 to build. It will lower its legs to the bottom of the Gulf, then raise its deck to the height of a ten-storey building.'

We see frequent flares, and at night they are all about us and the sky is red. These are caused by the escape of gas from the oil wells. It must be allowed to escape or it may blow up the well. But if it is not set afire it may lie under heavy cloud cover and be a serious menace, exploding if someone drops a match. Therefore it is burnt – enough gas to serve a city going up in flames. It is an odd sight, these great tongues of fire rising from the sea.

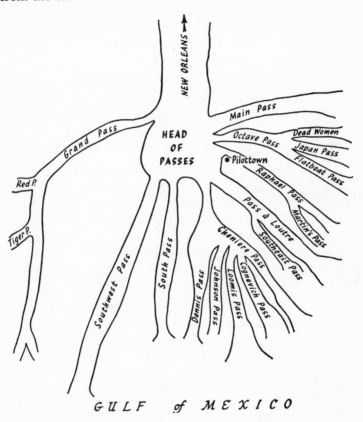

In a hydroplane of the Wild Life and Fisheries Commission we flew from New Orleans south over this strange watery waste, of which Mrs Trollope said that its horrors would have given Dante superb material for another *Inferno*. Following the river, we came at last to Head of Passes. Here the river splits up into many rivers, spreading out like the webbed foot of a duck, each pass finding its own way to the Gulf.

On Pass à Loutre we came down at the Wild Life Station.

It stands on a small wedge of land besieged by waters on every side and its few buildings are connected by cat-walks high enough to be clear of the cottonmouth moccasins. The station provides quarters for duck hunters and the region abounds in ducks, great white cranes, pelicans, nutria, marˑh deer and alligators.

Near by we visited Pilottown, an amphibious settlement perched on stilts where pilots stand ready day and night. They are divided into two camps. In one house are the river pilots and in another the bar pilots. They are friendly enough, but they have little to do with each other. They are two separate aristocracies.

The rules are strict. A ship must have a bar pilot below Head of Passes, a river pilot above it. We went out in the pilot boat to a ship arriving from the Gulf. A river pilot climbed aboard her and the bar pilot, his duty done, came down the ladder to our boat and was taken ashore. The river pilot would take the ship as far as New Orleans. Still other pilot associations take care of service on the river above New Orleans. It is not as crazy as it sounds. Each part of the river has its own problems and requires its own experts.

*   *   *

The river has been more than a hundred feet deep all the way down from New Orleans. Now it has become very tired. It is dropping its load. It comes up against the sediment that it has laid down itself.

This is, in a sense, the end of the river. This is point zero. Mississippi mileage is counted from here.

But a river can hardly come to a dead end. The waters still have to reach the sea. So, from Head of Passes or near it, they set out in all directions over the age-old river deposits, seeking the Gulf. Some of the channels are Main Pass (which is by no means the main pass), Octave Pass, Dead Women Pass,

Raphael Pass, Martin's Pass, Pass à Loutre, Seven Pass, Scarabin Pass, Contrariete Pass, North Pass, Grand Pass, Tiger Pass, Red Pass, Twenty-Seven Pass, Flatboat Pass, Southeast Pass, Cheniere Pass, Loomis Pass, Johnson Pass, Dennis Pass, South Pass and Southwest Pass. The two last named are most used. They have been 'stabilized' – so engineered that, with frequent dredging, they provide a thirty-five-foot-deep access to the sea.

We flew down the twenty-mile Southwest Pass to the Gulf. The tang of salt water was strong. Gulls, terns, cranes and pelicans filled the sky. But the mighty Mississippi was not done. Beneath us for miles out into the sea the water was brown, divided sharply on both sides from the blue. Flying fish and porpoises dashed into the fresh water and back again into the salt.

Gradually the colour faded and the last grains of soil from Montana and Pennsylvania were laid down. The 'Big Sewer' pours into the sea about a cubic mile of mud a year. No wonder the area of Louisiana is steadily increasing.

Has the great, temperamental, erratic, murderous river finally been licked? Perhaps not. Some old-timers say it never will be. But the effort is worth while. It is estimated that, since 1927, flood control has prevented at least $5,000 million in losses, not counting lives. The conquest of the Mississippi has been called 'one of the most ambitious undertakings ever conceived by man'. The success of this mammoth project to date has given valley dwellers a new confidence – in some cases a dangerous complacency. No doubt the river still has many tricks in its bag. Nothing but eternal vigilance will checkmate the infernal ingenuity of Old Al, the River King.

Index